Smouldering Incense, Hammered Brass

A Syrian Interlude

by

Heather Burles

TURNSTONE PRESS

Copyright © 1999 Heather Burles

Smouldering Incense, Hammered Brass
published by
Turnstone Press
607–100 Arthur Street
Winnipeg, Manitoba
R3B 1H3 Canada
www.TurnstonePress.com

Turnstone Press gratefully acknowledges the assistance of the Manitoba Arts Council, the Canada Council for the Arts and the Government of Canada through the Book Publishing Industry Development Program.

Le Conseil des Arts | The Canada Council
DU CANADA | FOR THE ARTS
DEPUIS 1957 | SINCE 1957

Canada

Some of the names and details in this book have been changed to protect people's privacy.

Printed in Canada by Friesens for Turnstone Press.

Original cover art and map by Ray Dirks

Design: Manuela Dias

Author photograph: Sharon Toochin

Canadian Cataloguing in Publication Data

Burles, Heather, 1957–

Smouldering incense, hammered brass: a Syrian interlude
ISBN 0-88801-237-3

1. Syria—Description and travel. 2. Burles, Heather, 1957–   I. Title.

DS94.6.B87 1999   956.9104'2   C99-920162-X

A NOTE ON SPELLING

There is no standard method of transliteration from the Arabic script to English. Arabic sounds unknown in European languages, combined with the fact that most vowels are not written, make it nearly impossible to agree on one method of transliteration. This book follows the simplest spelling of a word or a spelling that conveys best its sound in Arabic.

To mom & dad

acknowledgements

Thank you, thank you to Denise Lawson for commenting on drafts and for friendship through every stage of this book; Sheri Henderson for a "handy, helpful handbook" and for remembering; my mother, Mary-Jo Burles, for commenting on early drafts and for Biblical research, and my father, Robert Burles, for his knowledge of horses and local history; my sisters, Jacquelyn and Gillian Burles, for commenting on various drafts and assuring me they would buy (and read) the book; my writers' group who supported my efforts through numerous drafts—Ellen Liberman for a wealth of ideas, Fiona Marks for a poet's sense of rhythm, Alan Patola for recognizing and confirming the joys of travel in the Middle East, Margaret Eriksson for insisting I face fear, and Deborah McDonald for pushing me beyond early endings (and Stephane for early encouragement); Margaret Dyment for expert advice; Linda Nielsen for creative support; Isabel Nanton for lifting an internal veil; Marianne Bos for giving me direction; MDA Toastmasters for offering a place to grow "paper wings," and MacDonald Dettwiler for allowing me to slip in and out of the traces; Sharon Toochin for understanding light and taking the time to capture it; Manuela Dias, Managing Editor at Turnstone Press, for guiding me through the world of publishing while turning a manuscript into a book; Armin Wiebe for editorial wisdom and encouragement; Ray Dirks for creating watercolour magic for the cover; and special thanks to my partner Gerd Sandrock for time and space, both in Vancouver and in Hay River. And *shokran* to the people of Syria, *habibi sagheer*, and especially Offa and Ahmed and Huda. Thank you, thank you. *Shokran.*

part one
interlude in Damascus

One-Way Ticket 3

I Take This Man, I Take This House 13

A Reprieve 19

No Dogs in Damascus 25

Welcome 27

Offa 33

Dawn in Damascus 41

A Formidable Language 45

Good Woman on the Mountain 49

Desert Festival 53

Invitation to Tea 63

Corporate Blasphemy 67

After Tea 69

Bludan 73

Something Funny 75

Expatriate Scandal 79

Laundry 81

My Godmother 83

Survival 87

In the Hands of God 89

I Wish 91

Ululations 93

Watercolour Days 95

part two
Syrian sorties

Travels with a Man 105

Expectations 109

Whirlwind Tour 111

Summer 117

Visas 119

Quneitra 121

A Night in Dara'a 129

I Remember Moona 139

Fear 143

A Deliberate Accident 147

Travellers 153

Sightseeing 157

A Damn Good Place 163

Sanity & Saints 167

Trees 169

Kafroon 173

Books 175

Farewell 179

"In spite of dust, noise, tawdriness, ugliness of detail, there is magic: not to be understood in a day or even two!"
— Freya Stark, *Letters: Volume One*,
18 March 1928, Damascus.

part one
interlude in Damascus

▩ one-way ticket

At the age of thirty-seven, I bought a one-way ticket to Damascus. I had never been to Syria and I didn't know anyone who had. But after five years of designing and developing computer software, I needed a break. I like to travel, I had studied some Arabic, and also I'd bet my sister I could learn to ululate. One can always dredge up reasons, but I believe the real reasons often lie so deep in the well, they may never come to light.

My itinerary was vague: gallivant around Syria for a month or two, and then my lover, whom I was leaving behind in Canada, would join me for a month's holiday. He would return home and if I was tired by then of travelling, I would study Arabic for a while; if not, I would head somewhere else— someplace cheap that would grant me a visa.

I purchased a map of Syria with what looked like five o'clock shadow flecks depicting "stony desert." Green borders held Turkey, Iraq, Jordan, Israel, and Lebanon at bay. Only the Mediterranean coast, facing a sea of blue, was free. In the north was the Euphrates, a shocking blue worm wriggling across a pale expanse of yellow. In the south a grey splotch represented Damascus. Roads, paved with either blood or gold if the colours on the map were accurate, tied the capital city to other splotches (Beirut, Aleppo), and to small circles and dots like Zabadani, Deir az-Zur, and Raqqa. On the flip side of the map was a blown-up version of the capital city, Damascus, a patchwork quilt of mint-green parks and rose-coloured built-up areas.

I bought a Middle East guidebook and used it to choose a "bottom end" hotel, well away from the area where it said hotels double as brothels, and the airline booked a room for me. I glanced at "Things to See" just long enough to convince myself and anyone who asked that there are tourist attractions in Syria. Unless I'm within a camel ride of the topic at hand, I find reading guidebooks tedious.

At the Vancouver airport I discovered the hotel had confirmed "a bed in a shared room for him."

"I'm not a him!"

The airline clerk agreed and promised to rebook. By the time I reached Amsterdam, the confirmation read: "a single room for a lady."

It wasn't the first time I had gone off travelling and although some people thought I was crazy, middle age had actually made me rather sensible. Not only had I booked a room, I had even arranged to spend a few days with friends in Belgium to recover from jet lag before carrying on. I hadn't bothered to do either of those things at age thirty-two when I flew into Cairo alone at three in the morning, suffering from transatlantic jet lag as well as a wicked head cold, an untreated urinary tract infection, and diarrhoea left over from a three-week vacation in Haiti. (I never buy flight cancellation insurance because I figure if I'm too sick to be on the plane, I'm dead.)

As a result of my middle-aged prudence, I arrived at the airport for the final leg of my journey to Damascus healthy and well rested. I sat down in the lounge, leaving three empty seats between me and a young woman in a long blue dress and a woollen headscarf patterned with horses and hounds, yet her daughter, who looked to be about five, made a face at me. I wondered if that was a bad omen. A hundred grams of chocolate eggs filled with Grand Marnier helped me push back anxiety as I watched the girl and her brother play at hiding his bottle. Since Islam forbids alcohol, there was no reason to share the chocolates.

When the flight to Damascus was called, a woman in a tent-like black robe preceded me down the accordion hallway connecting the terminal building to the aircraft. To me, that woman represented the Middle East—mysterious, exotic—but then, at a bend in the hallway, a gust of wind billowed her robe, and for a moment she seemed demonic.

What am I doing going to Damascus? I thought as I took my seat for the final leg of my journey. In front of me, above the tangerine-coloured blotting paper on the headrest, was a woman's tightly scarfed head, a half-circle of brown and black wavy streaks, a camouflage pattern of protective colouring for mud ducks in dry grass habitats. She fit in. I didn't. What was I doing going to Damascus? To block out my thoughts, I read the *International Herald Tribune* from cover to cover, skipping only the articles about terrorism.

When I had finished the paper, I looked around and discovered the woman beside me wasn't wearing a scarf. Jane was an Englishwoman with shoulder-length stringy blonde hair, a pale complexion, and clear grey eyes. She was on her way back to Damascus from England where her children were in boarding schools. She smelled like toffee. Her husband worked in the oil industry in Syria and they had been living in Damascus for two years.

I told her about my vague travel plans and the possibility of studying Arabic. "Have you learned any?" I asked.

"*Shokran* (thank you), *bikam* (how much), a few numbers. There's no reason to learn Arabic. It's a difficult language and you can get by in English." She tucked a tissue into the sleeve of her cardigan. "How long will you be in Syria?"

"I don't know. A few months, maybe. See how I like it."

Jane looked puzzled. "What type of visa are you travelling on?"

"Tourist, multiple-entry."

"You can't stay longer than six weeks, possibly eight, no more."

Visa extensions—I hadn't given them much thought, but I wasn't ready to admit that. "I'll just leave the country and come back."

"You can try." The look on her face said I was being naïve.

"Do you have a work visa?" I asked. Her children were in boarding school, presumably her husband worked all day, and she certainly wasn't learning Arabic. What did she do all day?

She rolled her eyes and snorted. "I would never work in Syria. The wages are so low, it would be financially ruinous."

Dinner came with a card, saying in six languages: *This meal does not contain any pork or any pork extracts.*

Jane told me where I could change money in the gold *souq* and what rate to expect on the black market. She also told me Damascus was very safe and that she loved living there. After the dinner trays had been cleared away, she wrote down the names of restaurants, and advised me not to order anything without first asking the price. When she handed me the list, she told me again how much she loved living in Damascus.

"Do you have much contact with Syrians?" I asked.

"No," Jane said, shaking her head, "we socialize with other expatriates. Our standard of living is so much higher than that of the locals...." I wondered whether I could afford the restaurants she had recommended. A moment later, she added, without a trace of regret, "Besides, it's impossible to meet Syrians—because of the language barrier."

It was dark when we landed. I had known it would be.

Jane's husband was meeting her, but she didn't offer a ride and I didn't ask. Her last words to me, called out in the crush of people lining up to leave the plane, sounded like: "Don't eat the lettuce."

I never saw her again.

A man at the airport transportation desk said he knew the hotel I had booked, and after taking a whopping twenty American dollars and writing my name and passport number in a spiral-bound book, he handed me over to a heavy-set driver who locked my backpack in the trunk of a Mazda taxi and put me in the back seat. The driver had broad shoulders and wavy black hair. He lit a cigarette and switched on the radio. Smoke and Arabic music filled the cab as we drove down the middle of the road, speeding past billboards advertising the virtues of Iran Air, and the Syrian President, Hafez al-Assad. Dots of light in pools of darkness. On either side of the nearly empty highway, dusty pine trees looked like paintbrushes.

We didn't speak until the city lights came into view. Then the taxi driver wanted to know where I was going. He had never heard of the hotel. I fished a pen and a photocopy of the map in my guidebook out of my coat pocket, and circled the appropriate dot, saying it was close to Takieh as-Sulaymanieh Mosque. The guidebook didn't provide a street name.

When the city began in earnest—bleak concrete blocks had pushed aside orchards and pine trees—the driver pulled over to the side of the road and looked at the map, slowly running his nicotine-stained fingers over the English transliterations of the street names. I leaned over the seat and tapped my pen on the dot I had circled. "*Funduq.*" Then moving to a nearby dot, I added, "Takieh as-Sulaymanieh." While my pen shuttled between the two, I repeated, "*Funduq* Salam . . . Takieh as-Sulaymanieh," three times.

"Good, good," he said, tapping his yellowed fingers on the *funduq* and the mosque. "*Funduq* Salam . . . Takieh as-Sulaymanieh."

Then he accelerated fast and didn't slow down until we took the exit ramp near a mosque crouched like a bulbous spider. Lime-green neon lights encircled the minarets. It was after midnight, but a couple of shops displaying rows of shoes and brightly coloured beads were still open. The driver got out and spoke to a group of middle-aged Arab men—dark eyes, dark skin, dark hair, dark clothing—who stared at me: the bare-headed foreign woman in a red jacket sitting in the back of a white Mazda taxi in downtown Damascus late on a March Monday night.

The driver returned to the car and, after reversing quickly, we pulled into an alleyway. The walls of decaying buildings whizzed by. Where was he taking me? Peeling walls forced us left. Another alley. More of the same. What had he told those men? A right turn. Then we screeched to a halt. Worn steps and an unlit sign marked the *funduq* Salam, which the driver had found in a back alley.

Returning my map, he patted the paper, then covered the *funduq* dot and its blue circle with his yellowed index finger, and said, "Good, good." For a moment I thought he was recommending the hotel, but then I remembered he had never heard of it.

The hotel door was split down the middle but only the right-hand side opened because the left side was deadbolted to the floor. My backpack stuck in the narrow doorway until the taxi driver set me free with a push from behind.

The desk clerk, a small man with a narrow face and close-set eyes, wasn't expecting me. "Next week. You come next week," he muttered. I showed him my ticket—as if my being there wasn't proof enough that I had indeed arrived—and he removed his clothes from a double room beside the desk and gave it to me for the price of a single: one hundred fifty Syrian pounds, or three U.S. dollars.

The room was small and windowless, and the carcass of an inch-long burgundy cockroach lay in one corner. There were three doors at floor level—metal beds blocked two of them—and a fourth, about eight feet up one wall, led into mid-air.

The toilets were down the hall. The hole-in-the-floor pit toilet stank of urine, and the throne toilet, clogged with a log jam of excrement, smelled much worse. I prepared for the pit by tucking my pant legs into my socks because I thought if my pants touched the floor in the toilet while I was squatting, I would have to abandon them and sneak back to my room in my underwear. I made it back to the room with my pants on.

In the lobby the desk clerk set up a cot under a three-dimensional plastic image of President Assad. Within a few minutes he was snoring.

I lay awake for a long time, staring up at spears of light that outlined the door leading nowhere. The room was cold and I lay on the bed in my sleeping bag, trying to remember what it was I liked about travelling. The first night is always the hardest and I regretted not rationing the chocolate eggs.

The next morning I moved to a single room for a lady—a room with a bed, a writing table, a wooden chair, a filthy sink, a cracked mirror, a barred window, and only one door. The sun was shining and I set out with a map and a compass to explore the oldest continually inhabited city in the world.

The sound of typewriters clacked into the side street that led from the hotel down to the main street. An old Arab woman in a long black robe steadied a blue pail of leafy greens on her head. Garlands of glittery beads wreathed the cab of a Toyota garbage truck that left a trail of invisible putridness in its wake. A dusty gold, round-shouldered mountain—Jebel Qassioun, according to my guidebook—formed a backdrop for the sun-lit palms and the faded zebra-stripes of the Takieh as-Sulaymanieh Mosque, built on the bank of the Barada River by a Turkish architect in 1554. A man on a bicycle whistled like a tropical bird to warn pedestrians to get out of his way.

The downtown streets were full of people—mostly male people—whose eyes followed me. I was a curiosity. To them, the woman my eyes followed—a woman with a black cloth draped over her head and shoulders—wasn't unusual. She wore a navy blue raincoat, dark stockings, and black shoes with medium heels, and she walked arm in arm with a man in his forties wearing a business suit. If I were to raise the cloth, I wondered, what would I find? A tasteful display of diamonds and pearls under glass? Or the head of a fly on a woman's body? Perhaps she was having a bad hair day. As a pimply teenager, I might have welcomed the opportunity to wear a rag over my head.

Behind the Foreign Exchange counter at the bank, four heavily made-up women with waist-length thick black hair chatted as they ate pizza. I suspected the weight of their gold jewellery forced them to move slowly. I cleared a path through the books and binders littering the counter. After a few minutes the women had finished eating, and one wiped her fingers on a napkin, brushed her hair out of her eyes, and cocked her head, ready to serve me. Her hoop earrings were big enough to be bracelets. She took my passport and filled out forms while her three colleagues peered into compacts as they proceeded to touch up their lipstick. I changed just enough money to get an official receipt in case the hotel should ask to see it. A balding man handled the actual bills, while behind the counter, the woman who had served me raised a crimson stick to her lips. At the back of the bank, a woman in a pink headscarf pressed a white telephone receiver to her muffled ear.

The downtown streets were also full of traffic—honking, stinking trucks and busses and cars. To cross a street, I joined pedestrian crowds, large enough to intimidate drivers who hesitated to plough into us, probably because the number of ribs and collarbones increased the likelihood of puncturing a tire. Crossing ath-Thawra Street, near the main covered market, the *Souq al-Hamidiyyah*, I was at the back of a group when the driver of a yellow taxi decided he had waited long enough and began inching his car forward. I put my hand on the hood and swung myself out of the way.

Cars can't enter the *Souq al-Hamidiyyah*. In the shadows of the *souq*, a paper caterpillar swooshed around the worn-out shoes of a boy who looked painfully bored manipulating the strings. All the way through the market, hawkers called out to me, "You want to see embroidered tablecloth? Oriental carpet? Beautiful silver? Please, I have Bedouin dresses, jewellery." As I walked past backgammon boards and belly-dance outfits, wind-in-the-grass whispers swept over the cobblestones: *Change money? Change money?* I went to the shop in the new gold *souq* the woman on the plane had told me about.

Then I wandered around the Old City, losing myself in a maze designed for warm-blooded modes of transportation. I squeezed a hand, a woman's hand, destined to serve out life as a brass door knocker. I listened to unshod hooves clop over the cobblestones and I smelled the warmth of a blinkered horse (and supposed it could smell me). I stood under an archway, my body cloaked in shadows, and reached out my hands to gather up sunlight. The Old City reminded me of life: in both directions, a street's trajectory is hidden. Though it comes from the past and leads to the future, only the present exists.

But I wasn't blinkered. The present faded as my mind leapt to tomorrow. What would I do? Visit a museum or a mosque? Or move on and come back later? How do you cram the oldest continually inhabited city in the world into a three-day itinerary? I let my mind roam aimlessly and by the time I had wandered onto Bab Sharqi Street, the biblical Street Called Straight, I realized I didn't actually want to travel, to lug my backpack from one grubby hotel to the next. I wanted to slow down, to be a part of something. I wanted to stay in Damascus.

In the weeks and months that followed, I discovered—neither the map nor the guidebook had told me—that in Damascus, grey plaster and concrete blocks pass for modern architecture; canals and rivers choke on garbage and run to hide under pavement; machine guns outnumber purses; and insecticide fogs roll through the streets, stinging eyes and throats and slaughtering columns of mosquitoes.

And I discovered that in Damascus, jasmine seeps into the air, enchanting all those who breathe; every fountain is a celebration and every park a garden; cherries and apricots rise out of the soil; doves whisper, and swallows pierce and embroider the sky.

◼ *I take this man, I take this house*

I've come close to marrying twice in my life. It won't happen again—at least not for a long time. *Till death do us part.* I would choke on those words. Only the very young, the naïve, or the very old can solemnly pledge undying devotion if murder is out of the question. If adultery and divorce are options, why bother with vows? They have no meaning.

It's ironic that I am named after a woman who married three times (once divorced, twice widowed), changing her surname like a chameleon as was expected when women were property. My grandmother signed her paintings, which she produced only in the interlude between her second and third husbands, with her first name, my middle name, Laurell. Her sister Maisie was a spinster, like me.

Muslim men are allowed four wives, which means spinsters are not common in the Middle East. Seven years before I went to Damascus, I visited Turkey, and in the Cappadocia region, a farmer, who had uncovered the entrance to an underground city while watering his tomatoes, had explained: in the country, pretty girls marry at fifteen, the not-so-pretty at eighteen; in the city, pretty girls at eighteen, the not-so-pretty at twenty. I was thirty then, apparently well past my prime, yet on an overnight trip along the south coast, I awoke to find the bus conductor's hand fondling my knee.

A couple of years later, in Jordan, I discovered that Arab men understood "I have a boyfriend" as *you are not married* and carried on in the pathetic hope (and eager expectation) that a western woman might behave like her celluloid counterparts. A twenty-five-year-old engineering student in Amman, who confided that he had had no experience with women, seemed profoundly shocked when I expressed a desire to return to my hotel room alone after a day of sightseeing. "You are not inviting me to your room?" It was a struggle for me not to laugh. At the citadel two days earlier, a man had grabbed me and pawed at my breasts.

Guidebooks advise western women alone in the Middle East to claim they are married. A husband, even an invisible one, provides a stamp of respectability and trespassing is *verboten*. I had managed without an imaginary husband in Turkey, Egypt, and Jordan, yet in Syria, I succumbed.

The secretary at a language school where I inquired about Arabic lessons knew of a house for rent and arranged for the owners, Ahmed and Offa, to show it to me. Ahmed was a short, silver-haired man who placed his right hand on his heart, closed his eyes for a moment, and bowed his head respectfully when he met me. His wife Offa was a squat woman with small eyes and a bulbous nose. Her skin was like whole-wheat bread dough and her eyebrows were brown-pencilled upside-down smiles. Both spoke English passably well.

"You married?" Offa asked, before we had even reached the house.

My lover was planning a holiday in Syria. To request that an unrelated man stay with a single woman would have been disgraceful, and I didn't fancy passing him off as my brother. No pledges, no rings, no vows—after a moment's hesitation a simple "yes" downgraded the status of my lover to husband. I hoped it wouldn't change anything.

"Your husband here?"

"No, he's in Canada." She didn't seem to find that odd. I found it disquieting that Offa and Ahmed accepted my invisible 'husband' without batting an eye. Did I really look like someone's wife?

The house was on the lower slopes of Jebel Qassioun, the camel-coloured mountain that overlooks Damascus. The entrance was at street level, yet the kitchen, at the other end of the former cabinet-maker's shop, was the third floor of someone else's house, and the kitchen window was at minaret level with a mosque on the street below. The garage-sized house shared a wall with a carpentry shop, and the air held fragrant undertones of wood and sawdust.

The current tenant hadn't moved out yet and Offa frowned at a pair of crumpled blue jeans on the couch, the unmade bed, a wrinkled shirt on the back of a chair, and at the dirty dishes covering the kitchen counter. "A boy live here," she said with an apologetic smile. "He is American. Nice boy, but not clean. A girl is better—more clean."

Since it was a small house and I didn't have much with me—just one pair of pants, a skirt, a pair of culottes, a sweater, two shirts, and one t-shirt—I figured I could probably manage to perpetuate the myth that girls are neater than boys by rounding up the clothes I didn't have on and chucking them into the wardrobe before opening the door if Offa came to visit. (I had no idea then how often she would visit.)

I liked the wee house, especially the bathroom, which was clean and smelled nothing like the one at the hotel, where I was the only woman and the only foreigner, and had settled for cold-water sponge baths at the sink in my room with my shirt hung over the keyhole in the door. But I didn't take the house right away because it cost three times more than the hotel. It

15

was also at least ten times nicer, but I'm incapable of snap decisions that involve spending money. I once slept on a piece of plywood for a year and a half after a tomcat rendered my mattress unusable.

Offa and Ahmed lived in a spacious high-rise apartment a few kilometres away and they invited me there for a meal. We ate rice, spinach-like *mulukhieh*, and fried spaghetti at the dining room table. China plates from Paris, Berlin, Brussels, and Amsterdam decorated the walls. The couple had been to Europe several times, but Syria was home. "In Damascus, we come from the heart." Offa's hands swept through the air and her face displayed what some might think was an indecent amount of emotion. Can a woman who has programmed computers ever come from the heart? I wondered. Possibly in Damascus, I thought, and I told them I would take the house.

A freckle-faced American man dropped by after we had eaten. Offa beamed when she saw him. "This is Dave!" she said.

Ahmed went into the kitchen to make coffee. Dave sat down in an armchair and Offa sat on the footstool at his feet. "He is like my son," she said. Her fingers were clasped as if in prayer.

Dave grinned at her and then turned to me to say, "It's a bittersweet experience."

"What do you mean?"

"If you hang around for a while you'll see. They're both really nice though." Offa continued to beam at him. Her smile never faltered.

Ahmed returned with a tray of tiny cups holding silt-like Arabic coffee. He explained to me that he and Offa had converted the cabinet-maker's shop into a small house for Dave, who had lived with them for two years, but then Dave had chosen to move into an apartment with a friend. So they had rented the house to an American studying Arabic who would return to the States in a few days' time. Ahmed said if I wanted, I could sleep on a cot in their living room until the house was empty.

"No, no. *Funduq* Salam is fine," I said. "It's near the Takieh as-Sulaymanieh Mosque. Very central."

"As you like," he said.

"I've never heard of it," Dave said. "How much are you paying?"

"A hundred and fifty pounds. Three bucks."

Dave guffawed. Offa looked horrified and she urged me to stay with them until the house was ready, but I was determined to maintain my independence. I had no desire to become like a daughter to her.

"As you like," Ahmed said again. "Damascus is safe. No problem."

The three of them gave me a ride back to my hotel. Dave pointed out a crest-shaped sign near the main post office on Said al-Jabri Avenue and warned me to look both ways before crossing the street. "Those are last year's scores for traffic accidents, including pedestrians injured or killed."

My hotel was near there and when we got to the Takieh as-Sulaymanieh Mosque, I directed Ahmed into the side street that turned into a back alley. "There's my hotel," I said. "*Funduq* Salam."

"Not so bad," said Ahmed, though he didn't sound convinced.

Dave said, "See you around."

Offa didn't say anything.

Moving day was a Monday, a week after my arrival, and something I had eaten the previous day—either pretzel bread or a vegetarian pizza (it couldn't have been the chocolate cake)—didn't agree with me. After throwing up in the sink and the trash can, I checked out of the single room for a lady and slumped on the couch in the lobby. Half an hour after Ahmed should have been there, Offa called to say he would come later, about four hours later. A good book, *The Republic of Love* by Carol Shields, made the time pass quickly.

I had finished my book when Ahmed arrived about one

o'clock. I still felt a bit queasy, but to move into the small house all I had to do was climb two steps and drop my backpack on the living room floor.

Ahmed showed me the portable electric heater, and demonstrated how to use the gas stove and how to turn on the hot-water heater, which dripped when it was on. He put a plastic basin on the floor to catch the drips from the red tank mounted above the kitchen doorway. And he instructed me to put toilet paper in the garbage can, not the toilet. The washrooms in the lobbies of four- and five-star hotels in Damascus had signs posted with the same instructions.

Before Ahmed left, he put the key in the door and said, "When I go, you lock the door. Turn the key, like so." He turned the key clockwise and we heard the deadbolt clunk. "You can leave the key in the door, but you must pull the key a little, like so." He pulled the key partway out of the lock. "Then we can come in. If we knock and you cannot open the door—maybe you are sick—we unlock the door from outside, we come in. We help you. No problem."

No problem! What if I didn't answer the door because I was in the shower?

He continued, "If you put the key like so," he pushed it all the way into the lock, "we cannot come in. So you must pull the key a little, like so." The key emerged from the lock.

"I understand."

Then Ahmed pointed to the peephole and said, "If somebody knock, you look here. You see me, you see Offa, okay, open the door. You see stranger—*no*—don't open the door."

He went out and came back a few minutes later with yogurt and ginger ale to settle my stomach. Then he left, saying to phone if I needed anything. I turned the key, heard the deadbolt clunk into place, and I pushed the key all the way into the lock. The hot-water heater was on and I hadn't showered in a week. But first I called Offa to ask where I could find something to read.

⊞ *a reprieve*

Arabic classes don't start in March but a student at a language school recommended Nabil as a private tutor. Nabil lived in Bab Touma, the Christian quarter at the east end of the Old City, farthest away from the clean waters and refreshing winds that come out of the mountains in Lebanon.

I had walked to Bab Touma from the hotel, but the little house was farther away. Ahmed wrote out the names of two *meecro* routes I could take, then he walked uphill with me to a main street where the *meecro* vans sped by. The routes didn't have numbers and the destination signs were only in Arabic, which made it difficult for me to flag one down, because unless traffic was badly snarled, it took me longer to decipher the destination than it did for the van to drive by. Ahmed flagged down a Muhajrin Shora *meecro* which connected with another route that took me to a mediæval gate—the Bab Touma quarter's namesake—a stone arch stranded on an island in a traffic circle.

I had time before my lesson, so I dodged the traffic and

skipped into the shadows of the mediæval gate where a juice stand hid behind string bags of oranges, bananas, and lemons. I pointed to what I wanted like a child in a candy store, then retreated to the grass beside the gate with a frosty mug of freshly squeezed juice. Sitting on cool grass and sipping juice through a straw, I reviewed my homework and pretended the myriad honks behind me were just geese gone mad. When I had emptied the mug, I returned it to the stall, then ran through the crazy geese and into the narrow streets of the Christian quarter where cars don't fit, so the world slows down.

In the Old City, I wound my way through a maze of shadows where wooden rafts cantilevered out over the street to support the upper stories of houses made of mud and straw. In places the skin of a wall had peeled away to reveal wooden skeletons framing mud bricks woven like tweed.

I walked by the corner store (a cubicle no bigger than a phone booth), past wrought iron gates guarding a stone church, and on past doors leading into courtyards where sunlight filtered through quivers of eucalyptus leaves and fired the purling waters of marble fountains.

I walked slowly, yet I got caught behind a donkey cart rattling over the cobblestones while its owner, with his head bundled in a black and white chequered cloth, hunched over the reins, shouting, "Oranges. Ten lire." His cries echoed over the click of the donkey's hooves and the clatter of the wagon wheels on the stones. Nestled in burlap in the back of his cart were bright little circles of gold.

It was impossible to pass the wagon. It took up the whole street. At a corner the donkey had to go backwards and forwards to patiently ease its burden round the bend. That was my chance to slip by, to continue on my way to Nabil's house.

Nabil's house was at the end of a skinny little street that went no further than his doorway. Inside the courtyard his mother was peeling potatoes. From the courtyard, an open-air stairway jackknifed its way to the roof where Nabil's room started a third floor. His windows looked out on church bells, treetops, and laundry hung out to dry.

His room was crowded with furniture: a table, three chairs, a bookcase, a couch, a double bed, and a bedside table piled high with books. In the middle of the room was an oil heater with a stovepipe that went up to the ceiling and cut across to the corner. A Swiss woman, a Persian scholar, had an Arabic lesson before mine, so I sat by the heater until her lesson was finished. When she left I took my place at the table with Nabil, who smelled of tobacco.

Nabil was twenty-eight years old, a dark-skinned man with tiny eyes and a bristling black moustache. He poured tea from a metal pot and we drank it from heavy glasses while we spoke of laughing boys, roosters on fences, and camels drinking —in Arabic, of course.

At the end of the lesson, Nabil, whose name meant "highly intelligent," asked me about the meaning of my name. Translating *heather* into Arabic from English might not have caused a problem, but I didn't know the translation and Nabil didn't speak English. When we weren't speaking Arabic, we spoke German, a second language for me and a third, after French, for him. So in German, I tried to explain the meaning of my name.

"*Heather* is a flower. A small, purple flower in Scotland. In German, it's *Heide*." Nabil didn't know the word. He handed me a German-Arabic dictionary, pocket size. I flipped through the pages, found the word *Heide* and showed it to him. When Nabil read the Arabic translation, his tiny eyes flashed and his dark skin paled. I remembered then that the German word *Heide* has two meanings, depending on whether it's used as a feminine or a masculine noun. The feminine meaning is *heather*, but Nabil's dictionary was small; it only gave the meaning of the masculine noun: *heathen*.

Nabil slammed the dictionary shut, threw it on the table, and stormed across the room to pull a German-Arabic tome from a bookshelf. Thumping it down on the table, he motioned to me to find the word. He stood beside me with his arms folded over his chest like an angry schoolmaster. As I flipped through the pages anxiously, I reflected that in Germany, when someone asked about the meaning of my name, I used to joke sometimes: "*Heide. Die weibliche Heide, nicht der männliche!*" The feminine, not the masculine. Apparently not a laughing matter in the Christian quarter of Damascus.

The big dictionary listed both the masculine *heathen* and the feminine flower, *heather*. Nabil was relieved; so was I. He drummed his fingers on the page below the entry listing my name. His eyes still held a shadow of horror, but his face relaxed, and he nodded and even smiled a little. I looked out the window past sheets and pillowcases hanging like lost souls, and my eyes caught hold of sunbeams cradling church bells. My parents hadn't named me Heathen: I had been granted a reprieve from damnation.

The Muhajrin *meecro* left downtown from a chaotic depot which gave me time to decipher the destination signs. I felt as if I had really accomplished something when I figured out which bus to get on without asking for help. On the way home, though, I realized I didn't know where to get off. I had just moved to Muhajrin the day before and Ahmed had driven me there by a different route. I didn't even know the name of the street where he had flagged down the *meecro* that morning. All I could remember was that on the north side of the street a fruit stand had a metre-long inflatable banana hanging from the ceiling. I scanned the street as we drove past vegetable stands and stationary shops and jewellery stores and barber shops and fruit stands and more fruit stands—what if they sold the banana or it sprang a leak? I thought—and not long after we had passed a padded cube where men, with their heads bent over their needles, quilted satin bedspreads, I saw a giant Chiquita banana swaying in the breeze. As we drove past it I realized I didn't know how to ask the driver to stop. I called out "hello" and waved my arms, and the driver looked at me like I was crazy, but he stopped the bus to let me off.

I walked back to the fruit stand, and bought an apple and a couple of bananas. The boy dropped the money I gave him into a bucket of crumpled bills. On the way out I looked up and whispered "*Shokran*" to the yellow Chiquita moon. Thank you.

🏵 *no dogs in Damascus*

Damascus is a cock crowing when sunlight pricks the horizon.

A white donkey draped in cauliflower baskets beside an old man in black pants with a drawstring at the waist and a baggy crotch that hangs down to his knees. A shy little donkey in a straw skirt with a man who sells handleless brooms in the early morning light.

A tired, dull horse dressed up to pull a water tank—turquoise beads and ivory shells matting its hackamore; a glittery red scarf hanging from its horse collar; ostrich plumes billowing from its forehead like charcoal smoke. A broken horse pulling a wagon decked in strawberry pyramids, its hooves scraping the uphill pavement as its master cracks the whip.

A camel's head hanging on an iron hook through its nostrils, with parsley shading lifeless eyes.

The sickly smell of sheep shit. A ram bleating on the sidewalk before the slaughter. A bloodstained fleece drying on a line. The slime of sheep intestines, and blood spilled on the sidewalk like a vat of wet nail polish.

A fluffy cat leaving a trail of red paw prints on a gritty curb.

A dog ... but there are no dogs.

"Why don't I see any dogs here?"

"Dogs are too noisy," Ahmed said, flapping his fingers against his thumbs to imitate barking. "If you see a dog, you must call the police and they come and take it away."

"Where do they take it?"

"They take it away to the mountains and set it free."

I suspected the police used the bullet-in-the-head approach Canadian ranchers use to deal with animals harassing cattle.

"No dogs? Car horns are noisy too."

"There are some dogs. Not many. They stay in the houses. Not on the street."

The call to the mosque was louder than any dog barking. *Allah akbar* coming from the loudspeaker on the minaret outside my kitchen window had jolted me awake at a quarter past four that morning. Islam must be some powerful religion to convince people to crawl out of bed at this hour, I had thought as my head flopped back on the pillow. Perhaps dogs had quibbled with the *muezzin* calling the believers to prayer. I sensed that Ahmed had said as much as he was going to say on the topic of dogs.

There are no dogs on the streets of Damascus.

✦ *welcome*

Huda replaced Nabil as my Arabic teacher because she was a woman, she spoke English (as a third language, after French), she lived close to my house, she knew Offa and Ahmed, and, unlike Nabil, she didn't put her hands on my arms or shoulders during lessons. She was around forty, petite, perfumed, with soft, rounded features and shoulder-length glossy black hair. She used lipstick and rouge, and subtle kohl produced a modern rendition of ancient Egyptian eyes. Huda wasn't married and her parents were dead so she lived with her brother and his wife and family. "Here a woman cannot live without a man. It's okay for you because you're foreign. A Syrian woman cannot live alone." She wasn't complaining. She was just stating the facts.

Huda was a history teacher, an elegant professional, who supplemented her income by teaching Arabic to foreigners. Every other day I had an early-morning lesson at her place. We sat at the dining room table, a formal carved affair with high-backed chairs and a matching sideboard full of exquisite breakables, and she served tea flavoured with eucalyptus leaves and cinnamon. We started in March when it was cold, and the oil heater crackled and stank and made me nervous. Later, in the spring, the heater was silent and she opened the windows. Sometimes we both stopped talking to listen to doves cooing.

Huda was an excellent teacher. She had a passion for her language and lessons with her weren't cheap. The cost of one was equivalent to five nights in a budget hotel. She hadn't known that such hotels even existed in Damascus. "Was it *clean?*" she gasped.

"So-so," I said, grimacing.

She shuddered.

I insulted her once by saying that Syria was a poor country.

"The Sudan is a poor country," she cried. "Not Syria!" We agreed to put Syria in a class of its own. "Not rich like Canada. But not poor! You can find everything here." She poured eucalyptus tea into delicate china cups. "Everything you want in every price range."

Huda wove history into her lessons. Did I know why the gold *souq* in the Old City was new (by Syrian standards) when the markets surrounding it were old? No, I didn't. I hadn't even thought about it and if I had, I might have insulted her again by suggesting prosperity. Dazzling displays of bangles and chains— all sold by weight—surrounded by water pipes, backgammon boards, and embroidered tablecloths.

"The French *bombed* the Old City," she said in a hushed voice, as if she were letting me in on a dreadful secret. "In 1925 French troops chose to destroy the most *populated*, the most *beautiful*, the most *historic* part of Damascus. This area we now call *al-Hareeqa*." The burning district.

Syria gained independence in 1946. A souvenir of the struggle, which ended in the evacuation of French troops, stood in Huda's parlour. "At that time, every house had one of these." She tapped her fingers on a shell cartridge with arabesque engraving. The metal casing was being used as a flower vase. Death mixed with the spicy scent of long-stemmed carnations.

Huda steered clear of more recent history: Arab-Israeli wars; the succession of military coups d'état ending with the Defence Minister, Hafez al-Assad, becoming president in 1971; uprisings, unrest; a brutal crackdown in 1982 that killed more than 10,000 people in the city of Hama; and tanks in the streets of Damascus when Assad's brother, Rifa'at, attempted a coup in 1984.

She also steered clear of religion, only mentioning it once. I told her how I had left my wallet in a *meecro* and fifteen minutes later, a man returned it to me in a graveyard before I had even noticed it wasn't in my pocket. The wallet was returned with not one lire missing.

"That's normal in Syria." Huda pointed at the ceiling. "People are afraid. Religion keeps people honest."

Yet, post-office clerks and shopkeepers would overcharge or shortchange me. Fruit and vegetables were cheaper if other customers were present when my purchases got weighed. And some taxi drivers—particularly the ones waiting near tourist sights—would forget to start the meter or claim it was broken and try to charge me three to ten times the normal rates. Huda could hardly believe the prices some taxi drivers tried to charge foreigners. "The driver must use the meter. It's the law!" she told me. "Threaten him with the police." Her advice got me yelled at and unceremoniously booted out of a taxi cab, and unfortunately, the worst insult I could muster in Arabic was: "You are not nice." Religion didn't keep everyone honest.

Whatever Huda's religious beliefs, she kept them to herself and I appreciated that. I wouldn't dream of wearing uncomfortable shoes, yet I've been known to force myself into the psychic equivalent of Chinese foot binding, crippling myself to avoid what I perceive might offend someone else. Keeping the laces on forever causes deformities, psychic fractures I'm unwilling to sustain, so eventually I confuse and disappoint myself as well as the person who unwittingly caused me to grapple with my desire to please. I didn't flaunt my own lack of religious beliefs but with Huda I didn't feel I had to pretend that I had any, either. I felt that I could walk in my own shoes. Huda was a secular oasis, a teacher, and a friend.

After I had been in Syria a few weeks, Huda said she wanted to ask me something: had the *mukhabarat* talked to me? The *mukhabarat* were "like police, but secret." She said they might come to my house.

"How do they know where I live?" On the forms required for visa extensions I put an area and the nearest post office. The house didn't have a street address. As far as I knew, the street didn't even have a name.

"They know where you live," she said quietly. "They know everything. And they might not say they are *mukhabarat*." If anyone asked me where I was learning Arabic, I was not to mention her name. "Say you're learning Arabic from friends. And don't talk about money—don't say you pay." Too late, I thought, if they know everything.

Mukhabarat wasn't in my dictionary, but the kh-b-r root formed the words for "knowledge," "report," and "to inform." Huda wasn't being paranoid when she said, "Someone is watching me." Seven inches of text in my guidebook were devoted to *Secret Police*. "They may be watching you too," she said. Surely they have better things to do, I thought. Yet I walked home with a new awareness of every pair of eyes on the street.

Letters from Canada normally took ten days. Two arrived in unsealed envelopes. The Canadian postmarks were more than a month old.

A knock at the door. Fish-eye view of a stocky man holding a clipboard. Don't open the door to strangers, Ahmed had said, so I hid behind the peephole until the man tired of knocking and went away.

Huda believed her phone was tapped. Sometimes mine rang in the middle of the night and when I answered, there was no one there—or, at least, there was no response. One night I could hear someone breathing.

Even though I assumed an innocuous Canadian passport would shield me from harm, my guard was up. I wasn't doing anything wrong, yet I began to doubt everyone. Huda's anxiety was contagious. Everyone was suspect and subject to scrutiny: where did we meet? how did we meet? what have I told you? Every conversation ran through a sieve of silent questions: are you telling the truth? what are you asking? why do you want to know? The question "Why would he lie?" was worthless.

It was like seeing the underside of a beautiful embroidered cloth. The tangle of threads was innocence lost. Welcome, I thought. Welcome to Syria.

Huda lifted the cloth.

🔲 *Offa*

The day I met my landlady, Offa, I wrote in my journal that she was a "short, happy (or at least smiling) woman." I don't remember anything that would account for this cynical parenthesis, yet unconsciously I must have seen behind the mask.

The day after I moved into the house, she turned up at my door for tea. I had no sugar so she accepted apple juice and sat down on a stool in the kitchen. She set her juice on the stove and leaned towards me with a childish look of excitement that seemed a bit ridiculous on a middle-aged face. "What you name your first son?" She knew I had no children.

"Offa," I joked. "She will be a girl and I will name her Offa."

She reproached me with a frown. "How long you married?"

"Two years," I said. It seemed like a good number, though I hadn't even known my lover that long.

"You see doctor?"

"No."

Offa was in her early fifties, had married Ahmed at nineteen, and, despite visits to fertility clinics in Europe, had no children. A tragedy. "If God give me five children, everything okay. But He don't," she whimpered and her face collapsed into a pathetic frown. "But Dave is like my son," she said and her face brightened. I remembered the freckle-faced American I had met at her place. He had said something about 'bittersweet'. "I love Dave *very very very* much." Offa's tongue flapped over the r's. "I pray to God to give you a son." I nearly choked on my apple juice. I didn't have the heart to confess I'm childless by choice.

The next day Offa brought white sugar in an apricot jam jar and we drank hot, sweet tea in the living room where a portable electric heater worked hard to banish the remnants of winter. My fingers curled around a warm ceramic mug. Offa took one sip of tea and put it aside, just like the day before. This time she pressed the palms of her hands together and, with a quarter-moon smile of joyous devotion, leaned towards me and asked, "You love Jesus?"

"A little," I said lamely, not wanting to offend—*no* seemed too harsh—yet not wanting to mislead, either.

"I love Jesus *very very* much." She spoke with a passion I reserve for sex or chocolate. Since Jesus is just another prophet to Muslims, I assumed she was Christian.

I finished my tea, but Offa barely touched hers and before she left, she waved her hand at the full cup and asked accusingly, "Why you not buy Lipton?"

"You don't like the tea?" I didn't want to tell her I had bought the cheapest tea I could find.

"Lipton is better."

Later that day Ahmed delivered Lipton's tea bags. "Maybe you have guests," he said.

A week later Offa told me how grateful she was that Ahmed had neither divorced her nor taken more wives.

"Are you Muslim?" I asked, feeling confused.

"Of course!" Offa didn't cover her hair, but television announcers and middle- and upper-class Muslim women often don't. She read the Koran, yet complained that her husband wouldn't allow her to attend church. I was thoroughly confused. "I love Jesus *very very* much because Dave is like my son," she explained with delight. "My mother is *very* angry if she know I read the Bible. I don't tell her."

Dave was in his mid-twenties, had reddish-brown hair, and was a devout Christian. He worked in an import business, studied Arabic, and had rented the spare bedroom in Offa and Ahmed's apartment. He read the Bible daily and Offa began to read it with him.

After living with Offa and Ahmed for two years, Dave had moved into a two-bedroom apartment with a friend. Offa told me how she had cried for three days and couldn't sleep. "I go crazy," she said, referring to that miserable period. Dave was the only one who could make her happy and Ahmed invited him to eat with them two or three times a week. Offa complained that sometimes he only came once a week, yet she beamed like a child whenever he was around.

Offa dropped by my house often—almost every day—and I soon became aware that Jesus and Dave were the only conversation topics that interested her. She loved Jesus *very very* much and Dave *very very very* much.

"Does Dave ever read the Koran?" I asked her once. He was, after all, studying Arabic and by the time I met Offa, he had already been living in Syria for three years.

"No. Why he read it?" she asked in wide-eyed amazement.

A woman turns herself inside out for a man while he carries on with his life. Of course, it was Offa's choice to read the Bible with Dave. Yet his lack of curiosity about her religion while she submerged herself in his made me furious.

Dave could do no wrong—until he announced plans to do an MBA in the United States. Even though he intended to return to Damascus, Offa became frantic. How could she survive without Dave? Would he promise to phone her from America every day? She had money, she would pay! No. He refused. He would phone her once a month. No more. Offa cried and cried and couldn't sleep.

Then she began plotting, scheming, conniving. She could improve her English. A student visa. She would go to America to study English. But Ahmed didn't want to go. That was fine. She would go alone—in spite of the fact that she had never gone anywhere by herself. Not even to Aleppo.

At this point, Ahmed begged me to talk her out of it. "Please," he said. "You are from Canada—near America. You are a woman. Maybe she listen."

I tried. Offa pounded her fist on my table and spat out, "I will go to America. Anybody say no, I don't care. *I will go.*" Then she started to cry. I brought her tissues, and she wiped her eyes and her bulbous nose. She balled the tissues up in her right fist. "Maybe you don't believe me," she said, "but Jesus talk to me."

"I believe you." Anything seemed possible in Damascus.

"If Jesus say, 'Go to America,' what can I do? I love Ahmed *very very* much. He is my husband. I love him *very very very* much. I don't want to leave my husband, but if Jesus say, 'Go with Dave,' what can I do? I must go."

"What if Jesus tells you to stay here with Ahmed?"

With a vehemence that scared me, Offa hissed, "He not say that."

How convenient! She had abdicated responsibility. Jesus told her exactly what she wanted to hear. And who could argue with Jesus? Certainly not a Canadian woman who only loved Jesus a little.

"I tried to talk to Offa about America," I told Ahmed when he drove me to the Immigration Office to extend my visa. "It's no use. She won't listen to me. I don't think she'll listen to anybody." Except Jesus, of course, but I didn't mention him.

Later that week Offa brought calendars from American colleges to my place and browbeat me into dictating letters for her. I helped her fill out application forms. "Divorced or married?" she asked. "Which is better? What you think?"

"Offa, you are married. This is a visa application. You *must* tell the truth." She would have done anything to get to America. Anything to be near Dave, who hadn't even left yet.

He caught wind of what she was doing and pleaded with her to give him some room. She refused. So he told her that wherever she went in America, he would go as far away as possible. If she went to New York, which was where he intended to go, he would go to California. If she followed, he would never speak to her again. He had to live his own life. "I go crazy," she whimpered.

At my place one afternoon she picked up a piece of bread that had fallen on the kitchen floor and ate it without even dusting it off. That wasn't like her. Offa scoured vegetables; I had seen her shampooing tomatoes. She was forever warning me not to eat just anywhere and had taken me around to the few "clean" shops in my neighbourhood. What was she doing eating off my floor? I didn't have that kind of floor.

"No matter," she said listlessly. "Jesus was poor. He ate dirty things. And next year maybe I'm dead." She went into the living room and I checked the valve on the blue canister of gas hooked up to the stove. In the journal she kept for an English class she wrote that she wanted to be buried in America.

A week later Dave left for New York and Offa was at my door with a pharmacology tome. "The doctor give me this." One finger jabbed a long Latin word. "For crazy? For crazy?" Her eyes pleaded with me.

The drug was listed as an antidepressant for acute mania.

"Not for crazy," I assured her. I noticed that her pencilled brows were unbalanced.

"Not for crazy?"

"No, not for crazy," I said gently. "It's for depressed people, for too much worrying, for thinking, thinking instead of sleeping."

She put the pharmacology tome on the table beside the

television and sat down on the couch in the living room. Her feet barely touched the floor. Her hands were cupped in her lap. She didn't move. She looked like a zombie. I broke the spell with peppermint tea and a strawberry tart, but conversation faltered.

For a few minutes the room was filled with echoes of mosques calling the faithful to evening prayer, the last of five daily prayers. *Allah akbar!* God is great! The echoes faded. I groped for something to break the silence.

"Is it ever a woman? Does a woman's voice ever call people to the mosque?"

Offa's head pulled back and her chin doubled. "Noooooooo." Her 'no' was even more emphatic and drawn out than the time I had asked whether it was possible to visit President Assad's Palace, which covered the top of a mountain and looked like a lion with Damascus under its paws.

Conversation faltered again.

I heard a drone like a low-flying airplane on the street below the house. The insecticide truck, belching out chemical poisons. I hurried around and shut all the windows before the white fog could stink up the house and tickle my throat.

"The mosquitoes are dying," I said when I sat down on the couch beside Offa again. I had brought her an orange and her fingers held it loosely. The weight of it seemed too much for her.

"Never mind," she murmured. "It's better that way."

"No more bites puffing up my eyelids."

She seemed to ignore my comment, but then it was as if she came to life. In a strong voice, she said, "From the mosque, it is *always* a man. *Never* a woman. *Never.*" She used a paring knife to cut through the waxy orange skin and her nails pried the soft-backed peel away from the fruit. "Heather, are you crazy?"

"Maybe." A long pause. The smell of the mandarin orange seemed to cheer up the room. "Aren't we all?"

"Never mind," said Offa, popping a section of orange into her mouth. There were tears in her eyes, maybe the orange was sour, yet she smiled. It had been a long time. She probably wasn't happy, but at least she smiled.

🔲 dawn in Damascus

In the nineteenth century, Alexander Kinglake wrote, "As a man falls flat, face forward on the brook, that he may drink, and drink again; so Damascus, thirsting for ever, lies down with her lips to the stream, and clings to its rushing waters." Damascenes claim theirs is the oldest continually inhabited city in the world. They call it *Dimashq*, or *ash-Sham*. The Prophet Mohammed turned away from Damascus because a mortal may only enter Paradise once. The city is built where seven streams push aside the desert and the al-Ghutah oasis creates paradise at the foot of a mountain. Jebel Qassioun. I love mountains. I woke up early one morning, long before day-break, and couldn't get back to sleep so I hiked up Jebel Qassioun. I sat on a rib of the mountain, amongst poppies like drops of blood, and savoured the stillness of the morning. Looking out at a mosaic of orchards, domes, and minarets, I thought about life trundling on and on, day after day after year after year. People caught up in the here and now as the past creeps up on tomorrow.

What of the past? If it weren't for the past, we wouldn't exist. Our lives emerge from a pool of ancient bones.

An example:

Me: A dead end. I have no children.

Parents: My father, a rancher; my mother, a writer. Both are full-blooded, alive. I know I'm lucky.

Grandparents: The ones I remember I clothe with flesh. My mother's mother wore big, big hats, made patchwork quilts and Tia Maria, and she was missing most of one finger. My father's father was the owner of goat angora chaps cut up for the beard of an old man in a school play. My father's mother sold a heifer she had received as a wedding gift to buy a Mason & Risch piano. She and her husband are buried under brome grass because grandma always said concrete would be too heavy.

Great-grandparents: Names and question marks written on the backs of sepia photographs correspond to stern faces, rigid bodies. Obviously they made love, but did they ever dance or laugh or even smile?

Ancestors—documented: Names, birthdates, ceased-to-exist-in-this-life dates, and *wife of* typed in black ink.

Ancestors—undocumented: Private, invisible lives. The empty list that overflows.

Sitting on the mountain, looking out at the oldest continually inhabited city in the world, I couldn't help but think about the forces of life that had come before the current inhabitants of the earth. A poppy, a cypress ... even an ant has ancestors. Do all the ghosts have room to play?

My grandfather Percy and his brother Tom homesteaded on the Snake Trail in Alberta's Porcupine Hills where I grew up. My great-uncle moved on some years after his wife left him with a school-aged boy at home, an infant son with neighbours, and a daughter buried in a grave now lost in the caraganas at the edge of the Cowley cemetery. My grandfather married

Elizabeth Yates, a Yorkshire woman, and together they raised one daughter and eight sons, along with workhorses and, later, beef cattle. I grew up playing in the corrals and horse barn he built, and exploring abandoned homesteads of men like the English bachelor, Henry Jackson, who wore white gloves to all the dances. "A gentleman," my grandmother had said. "A pity he drinks." He died in 1928, leaving his name on a quarter section. Others left theirs on creeks or buttes. Sam Tanner. Tanner Butte. Three generations of my family have watched the sun rise over Tanner Butte. A drop in the bucket. The teepee rings of the Blackfoot Nation remind us that we are not the first.

Somewhere above me, up higher on the mountain, a dog barked, and even though Ahmed had told me the police set dogs free in the mountains, I hadn't really believed him, and the sound startled me. Was it a ghost? Below me, on the roof of a concrete house at the edge of the city, a woman in a purple robe sat on a chair, breast-feeding her baby. A child of Damascus! I pulled the petals off a poppy and wondered how many hearts had felt the magic of dawn in Damascus as I watched the sun, crouched on the desert horizon, stitch tissues of light into the day.

◉ *a formidable language*

"Arabic is a formidable language."

I found it disconcerting that an Arabic teacher would say that. Huda loved her language and she was usually so encouraging to the poor sods who sought to learn it. Yet I had to agree. Arabic *is* formidable.

My first encounter with Arabic was in Cairo, some years earlier, when I deciphered the red and white billboards advertising Coca-Cola, thereby learning the Arabic letters for *K, O, L,* and *A*. I graduated to Nivea and Canada Dry. Back home, and moving beyond soft drinks and skin cream, I learned the rest of the alphabet from a *Teach Yourself Arabic* book.

I discovered that the *O* and *A* in Coca-Cola were long vowels. Short vowels—there are a lot of them in other Arabic words—are not normally written, because Arabic uses a 'defective' script. With the exception of the Holy Koran and children's books, where short vowels appear as scratches and squiggles above and below their more important brethren, only consonants and long vowels, liberally sprinkled with confetti-like dots, grace the page.

The placement of the confetti is of the utmost importance. It allows the reader to distinguish letters: a horseshoe with a dot over it is an *n*; the same shoe with two dots is a *t*; if the shoe is on top of the dots, it's a *y*; but if the horseshoe is sitting on only one little dot, it's a *b*. It's no different really than distinguishing a *t* from an *l* by the placement of a bow tie.

Capital letters don't exist in Arabic, yet each member of the alphabet comes in a few different forms because Arabic letters like to hold hands as they float across the page. Six renegades refuse to join hands with anything on their left, but otherwise the letters are a friendly lot. In order to be part of the parade, each one has four disguises: the isolated form when travelling alone, the initial form when leading the show, the medial form when caught in the crowd, and the final form where it unfurls its banners to bring up the rear with a flourish.

I learned all that from a book, and in Damascus, Huda marvelled at my handwriting: I had unwittingly learned to write like a typewriter. While reviewing the twenty-eight letters and their possible shapes, she taught me how to write like a person rather than a machine.

Whether typed or written longhand, Arabic consonants and long vowels parading across the page do so from right to left, making it seem that every book starts on the last page and progresses to the first. In reading, I wrestled with one word after another as my eyes inched across the page from right to left, and my hands hesitated each time I had to turn a page. But just when my eyes were finally going clickety-clack down the track from right to left, a string of numbers would derail me.

For some reason, Arabs write numbers from left to right. And to make matters worse, they don't use the numbers English speakers use and call Arabic numbers. The Arabs reach further East and use Hindu, or Eastern Arabic, numbers. Their zero is a dot, their five an angular zero, their four a backwards three, their two a backwards seven, their six a forwards seven, and so on. Toiling over the numbers, I began to feel dyslexic.

Yet, reading and writing Arabic were nothing compared to speaking the language. In Egypt I had learned some important phrases, such as, "Where is a pastry shop?" But otherwise I had learned my pronunciation in Canada and I had learned it from a book. I didn't know whether the queer sounds I made deep in my throat were those of Arabic, or whether, as my sister suggested, I really only sounded like a cow gargling.

Arabic has sounds that no European language has. To produce what linguists refer to as a *pharyngal voiced fricative*, Arabs use muscles English speakers only use to vomit. Although I speak German, I have never heard or produced a sound more guttural than the pharyngal voiced fricative. In textbooks, I've seen it transliterated as an apostrophe or a full colon, because no English letter can plumb the strangled depths of the Arabic consonant *'ayn*. To be sure that no student of the Arabic language could possibly avoid the formidable *'ayn*, it guards the fortress, standing proudly at the beginning of the word for Arabic.

Huda tutored me tirelessly in the correct pronunciation of her beloved tongue. She made tape recordings, which I listened to at home. I mimicked her as best I could, twisting my tongue and throat into unfamiliar postures. To produce the voiceless counterpart of *'ayn*, I pretended I was a whiskey-drinking cat, hissing. And for what linguists call a *voiceless uvular plosive*—what Arabs call *qaf*—I made those little choking noises heard in darkened theatres wherever popcorn is served.

I learned the grammar quickly. As in any language, the grammar rules are the steel girders that provide support for the bridge of understanding. What I found more difficult was gathering the words—the pearls, the beads, the sequins, and feathers—to turn the bridge into something more than cold steel.

I bought a pocket dictionary, which frustrated me by giving the Arabic for such a word as *phthisis*, yet leaving out *piano*. Searching for the meanings of Arabic words at the other end of the dictionary, I found that they clustered together like tribes. Words that have the same bloodline, or root, are listed in the dictionary under the first letter of the root, regardless of any prefixes. Thus *maktab* (office), *miktaab* (typewriter), and *takaataba* (to correspond) are all listed under *K*, because they belong to the *k-t-b* tribe that specializes in the idea of writing.

Between lessons with Huda I ventured into the real world of Damascus. I made a fool of myself at a concert by asking, "Am I famous?" And once I was photographing the ornate doorway of an otherwise plain house when the woman who lived there came home. "*Jameel*," I said. Beautiful. Then, in a hurry to put my Arabic lessons to good use, I impulsively plunged into a full sentence and accidentally boasted, "My house is beautiful." Embarrassed about having said something so arrogant, I rushed headlong into, "Your house is beautiful." She looked at me strangely as she pushed the door shut. I had addressed her as if she were a man. Only then, on my third try, did I finally say what I had wanted to say. To myself.

On the street one evening, I bent down to comfort a lost boy. His face was streaked with tears. "*Ma ismuka?*" I asked. Others gathered and asked him the same question, saying, "*Shu ismuk?*" What's your name?

The Arabic spoken on the street was not the same as that heard on the news, written in the newspapers, and studied in my lessons. No one spoke as slowly and clearly as Huda, and no one stayed within the narrow boundaries of my vocabulary the way she did. Yet, she pushed the boundaries ever wider, and under her tutelage I saw glimpses of the wonders of her language.

Huda was right: Arabic *is* a formidable language. But then Huda's French was better than her English. I wonder if she meant *formidable*[1].

---

[1] the French *formidable* means 'wonderful'

▨ good woman on the mountain

The road going up the south side of Jebel Qassioun is so steep the sidewalk crumples into stairs to keep up. Eventually the road abandons the straight-for-the-top approach to meander back and forth across the slope, and the stairs abandon the road to zigzag in tight little stitches between two rows of houses. The stairs end where the houses end; the houses end where the road peters out. That's the edge of the city.

On a Friday, the holy day for Muslims, I hiked up the mountain above Damascus. A greedy-eyed boy broke away from a group of teenage boys loitering at the edge of the city. The path was apparent but the boy insisted on leading the way. He huffed and puffed and had to stop for a cigarette. He sat down and patted the ground, inviting me to sit beside him, but I continued on, following steep erosion furrows up the side of the mountain. I only went as far as the roadside cafés, the highest point for civilians.

By the time the boy caught up, four women had invited me to sit with them on a wall outside a café. All were married and had children, even one I had thought was only a girl. The only child with them was a baby girl in a fuzzy sleeper that made her look like a pink rabbit. A woman with four gold rings—one was a snake—breast-fed the baby and then set her down in the dirt where she slobbered on pebbles her fat little hands held up to her mouth. After a while another woman picked her up and suckled the baby on her breast.

The woman with the snake ring had a wide smile and when she wasn't breast-feeding the baby, she bantered with the greedy-eyed boy who hovered around for a while. She had a beaded shawl draped loosely over her long black hair and her shawl often slipped out of place. After a couple of cigarettes the boy got up to go and he asked me a question—I don't know what he said—but all four women responded in unison with an emphatic: *La!*

No.

The brazen woman with the wide smile introduced me to her mother, a wrinkled woman in rainbow skirts, swishing between the plastic tables in a roadside café. A black scarf was pulled tight over her hair and forehead; a squiggly tattoo marked her chin. At first I thought she was begging. But then I saw how well-to-do couples in fine linens set aside glasses of tea and invited her to join them, how they leaned towards her with apprehension stretched across their faces, eager to catch her words, to hold them steady, to keep them from disappearing like the string of red beads—*click click click*—trickling through her fingers. Her golden bracelets jangled a warning. Sunflower seeds, pistachio nuts, and glasses of tea were forgotten.

The wrinkled woman sat with me for a while on the stone wall outside the café. Wisps of Halloween-orange hair with grey roots escaped from under her black scarf. She said I was a good woman, yet she shrieked in horror and nearly fell off the wall when she caught a glimpse of hair on my legs. Sticking a weathered hand under her rainbow skirts, she ran her knobby fingers over a smooth, hairless calf. Even the hair on my forearms made her grimace. With her eyes half shut, she made *smooth smooth* motions with her hand, then pretended to pluck hair from her arms, underarms, legs, moustache, brows (selectively), and even pubic area. By the time she finished, she was laughing, perhaps at the look of shock on my face. I didn't admit that in my unshaven legs I was an oddity. I left her with the impression that a Canadian woman wouldn't dream of removing body hair in a futile attempt to reverse the effects of puberty.

After that, I guess I must have been humming, because the fortune teller asked me to sing. I fumbled "O Canada" and brought it to a close early. Then "*habibi . . . habibi,*" the refrain of a song on a cassette I had bought in Egypt some years earlier. The woman cheered and joined in. Her breath was warm with garlic. We clapped and sang in seven-four time and she taught me a song I tried to remember, yet soon forgot. She never told my fortune; my Arabic wasn't good enough for that.

When I hiked back down the mountain, instead of returning the way I had come—I wanted to avoid the greedy-eyed boy—I followed a road switchbacking down the west side of Jebel Qassioun. The Presidential Palace was on the other side of the valley. I thought I was alone, yet nearly every time I stopped to attempt a photograph or even hesitated to evaluate a potential shortcut, there was a sharp whistle, and a soldier with a machine gun would appear among the terraced rows of cypresses and motion to me to *get moving*.

What might the fortune teller have told me? Take the long way home. There are no shortcuts. Your life is a string of red beads—*click click click*—trickling away. . . . Would she have told me to get moving? Or would she have suggested that I settle down?

I followed the main road home. The wind pulled at my skirt and whipped plastic bags into flight. I passed a man waving cartons of Marlboro and Pall Mall cigarettes at cars going into the city. By the time I got home my hair felt like dust.

51

▨ *desert festival*

English and Arabic posters advertising the third annual Desert
Festival of the Bedouin at Palmyra appeared in the windows of
travel agencies in the modern part of Damascus at least a month
prior to the event. With the narrow-minded arrogance of a
traveller who had been in the country for a whole six weeks, I
wrote it off as a tourist spectacle until two days before the
festival when I saw television advertisements featuring camel
races. Suddenly I *had* to be there. I rationalized that the Calgary
Stampede is not a tourist spectacle for the cowboys.

I tried to get a ticket for the festival, unaware the event
was free. And for some reason, no one in the travel agencies, the
tourist information office, or the Ministry of Tourism told me.
At the Ministry, a middle-aged woman with lacquered hair and
scarlet fingernails gave me a handwritten note and said a Mr.
Hamdi al-Arzha, the Chief of the Bedouin at Palmyra, would
"facilitate" things for me.

Huda recommended a hotel my guidebook listed as
"middle" and I resolved not to stay there unless all the "bottom

end" hotels were full. Offa called the tourist office in Palmyra and hung up the phone frowning.

"No hotel. Fool. All fool."

"Full?"

"All fool. Palmyra fool."

"Full." I was stunned. While I was dithering, others had snapped up all the hotel rooms.

"Palmyra not possible." She shrugged as if to say the conversation was over—she had done what she could to help me, the hotels were full, there was nothing more she could do.

"Maybe if I go there I can find a room...." I wasn't ready to give up. A *fool* Palmyra made the Desert Festival even more desirable.

"Hotel fool. All fool." She smiled at me the way you smile at a child after telling him for the third time there's no more ice cream.

"Well, I already have a bus ticket, so I might as well go," I said, formulating a plan as I spoke.

"Where you sleep? Hotel fool. All fool." She scowled at me.

"I don't know. Maybe I can find something. If not, I can take a late bus back to Damascus or go to Homs or ... something." I was smiling, excited and happy because I had a plan.

"Why make like this? Why you go?"

She was upset, and I could feel myself withdrawing from her. I wasn't asking her to go. Why didn't she mind her own business? But I kept smiling. I wanted my enthusiasm to win her over. "Don't worry. I'll pack light. I'll find something."

Ahmed patted Offa on the shoulder and told her I would be okay, though I could see my decision had shaken him, too. "Better you wait," he said persuasively. "You go later. Your husband come here. He take you."

My smile faded but my plan didn't change. "The Desert Festival isn't happening later," I said quietly.

"You go!?!" Offa leaned back in her chair, pursed her lips, and looked away from me.

When they rose to go, Ahmed said to Offa, whose eyes seemed to lock onto anything but me, "She is foreign." I suppose it was the only way he could explain why a woman would go off alone to a place where she knew all the hotels were *fool*.

The road from Damascus to Palmyra follows the route used in the olden days by camel caravans laden with spices, perfumes, and incense. The Syrian desert reminded me of tundra or prairie: an immense, introverted beauty not easily recognized by casual intruders. (I've heard the Subarctic described as "hideously monotonous.") Rocky desert is a landscape you learn to love slowly if you weren't born into it. After more than two hundred kilometres of browns and greys overlapping muted yellows, Palmyra, city of palms rebuilt by Solomon, was a refreshing sight. For Muslims, green is the colour of paradise.

A two-star hotel on the main street had vacancies but the rooms were expensive and foreigners were required to pay in U.S. dollars cash. In a bottom-end hotel beside a mosque on a side street, a bug-eyed Russian-Egyptian man, who claimed to have a Danish passport, had talked the owner into letting him deal with foreigners for the duration of the Desert Festival. Syrian pounds got me a bed in a room with three French women after I declined the cheaper option of sharing a room with the twenty-year-old acting manager.

Then I showed the note from the Ministry of Tourism to the local authorities, who muttered *kiteer sa'ab* (very difficult) while I feigned no knowledge of Arabic and looked at them expectantly. They advised me to wait and to come back later before finally suggesting I seek out the Bedouin camped a kilometre or so west of town.

Motorcycles and pickup trucks were parked at both ends of a white rectangular tent. Sky-blue poles propped up the roof. Men in *kaffiyahs*, the Arab headdress, and long loose robes called *galabiyyas* sat on thick carpets spread like a field of poppies and blue lupine on the desert floor. The tent was open to the east and when I approached, a hundred heads swivelled and a hundred *kaffiyahs* swayed.

I found Hamdi al-Arzha, a curly-haired, round-faced man, one of the few dressed in pants and a shirt instead of a *galabiyya*, leaning against an embroidered camel saddle at the back of the tent. Behind him were Syrian tricolour pennants—green, white, and black—and cotton portraits of President Assad and his handsome son Bassel, who had been a patron of the Desert Festival before he died at age thirty-three in a high-speed car accident in 1994. Hamdi was wearing a Bassel Assad wristwatch.

Beside Hamdi was the only other woman in the tent. Blue jeans, buttercup yellow blouse, lipstick, nail polish, designer sunglasses, streaked chestnut hair tumbling over her shoulders. Iman made English-language programs for Syrian television and was in Palmyra to do a show on the Desert Festival. I sat between her and a camel saddle, hanging my hat on the brass horn of the wooden A-frame with a padded cross-stitched seat. Iman smelled like jasmine.

After reading my note, Hamdi spoke to Iman in Arabic. Then in English as pure as crystal, she welcomed me on his behalf. I was his honoured guest: if I needed anything, if I wanted anything, the Chief of the Bedouin was at my service.

Iman asked whether I was a journalist and I sheepishly admitted that their honoured guest was nothing more than a Canadian tourist who had studied some Arabic. A boy brought glasses of strong black tea, saturated with sugar.

A Bedouin feast followed: bowls of yogurt; plates of salad greens, cucumbers, and tomatoes; and the *mensaf*—a communal platter of mutton and rice dotted with peas and pine nuts, and flavoured with sheep fat. Hamdi invited me to eat, saying, "In your honour."

The Bedouin men and I (Iman declined) squatted around the *mensaf* and right hands dipped into the food. A handful of rice and mutton, squeeze, tamp, pop into mouth. My companions made it look easy, yet I ate slowly, awkwardly, making a mess on the plastic cloth covering the carpet. I used a spoon for a salad plate and was working on a enormous serving of yogurt when Hamdi filled a plastic plate with rice and pieces of mutton, and presented it to me. He took a plate for himself, as well. The meat was tender and moist; I could cut it with the spoon. Everyone else continued to eat using the utensils they were born with. Once in a while a handsome Arab on my left broke his rhythm to toss a chunk of mutton onto my plate.

In the centre of the *mensaf*, crowning the rice mountain, was the skull of a sheep that hadn't been dead for long. The skull was still slimy and slick. The eye sockets were empty—a relief because I had heard tales of Arabs eating sheep eyeballs. The jaws were open, pointing straight up like a desert fox yipping at the moon, and pink swollen flesh protruded. One of the men said, in English, "You must eat the tongue." I thought I would rather eat the tongue of my own shoe lying in the dirt outside the tent. I turned to Iman and buried myself in English conversation with her. I was careful not to look at the skull again.

After I had eaten more than my fill, thanks to the handsome Arab throwing hunks of meat onto my plate, I moved away from the *mensaf*, hoping I hadn't offended my hosts by not finishing the bowl of yogurt. Someone took my place at the platter. He passed my yogurt around the circle for others to help themselves, using my spoon: what I had thoughtlessly regarded as mine had been intended for all to share.

A curvaceous brass coffeepot poured streamers of cardamom-laced coffee into tiny cups. A breeze billowed the tent wall behind me. Hamdi and Iman and several others disappeared, saying they needed to prepare for the races. A blue-eyed Bedouin man asked whether I could ride. I told him my father had five horses and that as a child, I had ridden every day, in the summer. He nodded his approval and I felt like a fraud.

I grew up on a cattle ranch in the Porcupine Hills of

Alberta. There were summers when my siblings and I rode every day, sometimes in our pyjamas, bareback through the caragana jungle before breakfast. But horses were only a means of transportation and we soon learned how to drive. Then the horses were only for work—herding cattle, round-ups, roping—and unfortunately, I left that work to my father and brothers, the cowboys. As a result, I never became a confident, or even a competent, horsewoman. I had barely graduated from Powderface, our beginner horse, when Piccina, a former pack-horse, ran away with me. Afraid that the Bedouin might try to put me on a feisty Arabian, I gripped an invisible steering wheel and quickly added, "Now I drive."

At the track, just east of the tent, horses far outnumbered camels—though you wouldn't know that, based on the pictures I took. Shot after shot of soft loose lips and bulging velvet eyes—the camels reminded me of Egyptian dowagers. The track smelled of horses and camels and haughty pride.

A stout man in a white *galabiyya* gave me apple juice in a foil pyramid with a stubby straw. "English! I speak English!" he said, slapping his chest. I asked him whether the races would start at four o'clock, which was what I had been told in Damascus. He laughed loudly before translating my question into Arabic for the amusement of everyone within listening distance. "I don't know," he chuckled. "Maybe early, maybe late. Never mind." Time dissolves in the desert. I didn't look at my watch again.

The bleachers were buzzing with Bedouin: girls in cobalt gowns; boys in t-shirts and jeans; men in *galabiyyas*, heads decked in red and white checkered *kaffiyahs*; old women in caftans and headscarves, faces lined with tattoos; and young women with babies wrapped up like papooses. There were a dozen tourists, mostly French, and hundreds of Bedouin. I saw Hamdi and Iman with microphones up on the announcer's platform. I stood at the white metal railing surrounding the kilometre oval of groomed red dust.

Using sticks, trainers coaxed the camels into a fuzzy line. Barefoot jockeys perched behind the hump, peeled stick in one hand, reins in the other. A pale camel at the far end of the line bellowed. Then they were off, with jockeys whacking them from above and trainers running alongside, beating them from below. The camels soon left the trainers behind, but otherwise they were in no great hurry; the stick-cracking arms of the jockeys were the fastest moving things on the track. The lead camel was the only one that even bothered to break from a trot into a gallop, and then only when it had rounded the final curve and was confronted by the roaring crowd brought to its feet by the excitement. The winner looked like a grotesque out-of-balance rocking horse as it loped across the finish line. There were no close contenders.

And there was only one camel race, yet I wasn't disappointed because the horses took their races seriously and I found them more exciting. In one race, a wild-haired man in olive green overalls rode bareback and his number stretched out behind him like a miniature cape. He leaned into the mane, dug the heels of his stocking feet into the horse's white gut, and shook the reins of the blue hackamore, urging the horse on to win. We cheered horse and rider all the way through a victory lap.

Every race had a few false starts and I never figured out who decided when the horses were in a line and what triggered the start. I never heard a starting gun, yet once they were off, it was in earnest. As the horses streaked by, necks stretched out flat, nostrils flared, tails streaming, hooves pounding the track into clouds of ferruginous dust, the Bedouins and I pressed against the fence surrounding the track. Police pushed us back and sometimes offered me, the foreigner, the newly cleared space by the railing, as if I deserved special treatment. I resented being singled out and refused to move back to the railing until the Bedouins did.

Once, after the horses had thundered by, I heard a

cracking sound and I turned to see three police officers—one with a peeled stick, one with a canvas strap, one with a chunk of wood—lashing out at the Bedouin crowd. I glared at the brutes, but didn't say anything. Afraid, I suppose, that I might *not* get special treatment. The Bedouins got out of the way; they didn't fight back.

After the last race, a tight knot of men formed around a plump, sandy-haired man and echoed his shouts. A canopy of fists waved *kaffiyahs* as the Bedouin from Hama in central Syria celebrated their winnings. The first prize purse was 150,000 Syrian pounds (the equivalent of three thousand U.S. dollars on the black market), a lot of money in a country where a hotel room cost as little as a hundred pounds. The men surged towards the announcer's platform, shouting, chanting, and punching the air. Police forced them back, and they hoisted a policeman onto their shoulders and moved onto the track. I was glad that theirs was a demonstration of joy.

During the awards ceremony, cameras flashed and triumphant music blared. A white horse held its head up high like a chess piece. Black tassels on the saddle blanket stood out against the pale hair on its belly. On the horse's back, in a cloth saddle with no stirrups or horn, was an old Bedouin man. His brown wrinkled face was framed by a red and white *kaffiyah* topped with a black cord. Bands of leather crisscrossed his chest, and a curved dagger hung at his waist. The old man held the hackamore reins firmly in one hand and a leather crop in the other. He sat tall in the saddle and sometimes he stood tall in the saddle, twirling his whip in the heavens above his head. The old Bedouin man reminded me of my father because he rode with an ease that only a man who has lived his life in the saddle can attain.

I looked for Hamdi and Iman after the races, but couldn't find them. Both the announcer's platform and the white tent were empty. I drifted to a nearby black tent where loudspeakers broadcast taped Arabic music while a man wailed what were presumably happy songs (I couldn't tell) into a microphone. A long line of men and even a few women held hands as they snaked and circled in front of the tent, hopping and stamping to the music.

As the sun went down, colours faded into darkness. A hawk-faced boy in dust-stained clothing poked sunflower seeds into my hand, and his face crinkled in happiness and pride when he told me the horses of the Bedouin from Hama were number one.

▣ invitation to tea

The morning after the Bedouin feast, I breakfasted on almond loaf and water shared with a boy in dirty jeans and a t-shirt outside the mud brick walls of modern Palmyra. We sat in shade cast by the ruins of the biblical city of Tadmor. Temple, amphitheatre, triumphant arch, colonnade, villas, tombs— ancient Palmyra fell when Queen Zenobia, a third-century warrior, dared to defy Rome.

The Bedouin boy pointed at his own little chest and, in English, said slowly and clearly, "My name is Helif." Then, pointing at me and beaming more encouragement than any English teacher, "My name is...."

"Heather," I said, dutifully playing the student by filling in the blank for him. At the sound of my name his face scrunched up. I said it again as slowly and clearly as I could. He looked as if my name were vinegar. In Arabic, I added, "Like the name *Hazaar.*"

"An Arabic name!" That tasted better. Then he switched back to English and slowly asked, "How many years?"

"Thirty-seven. *Saba'a wa talateen.*" I pointed at him. "How many years?"

"*Hidashar,*" he said proudly. Eleven.

Helif's teenage sister printed her name on my notepad as MTEF and told her brother she had written her name in English. I bobbed my head up and down. Fatima had written her name from right to left, leaving out short vowels, and the prongs of the *F* and *E* pointed to the left.

Their mother pulled over a piece of cardboard to sit on and joined us. "Um Helif," she said with her palm pressed against her chest. (She had become Um Helif, literally 'mother of Helif', when her oldest son was born.) Hennaed braids, loosely wrapped in black gauze, hung over her chest like ropes. A stiff peaked arch covered in black fabric crowned her head. Tapping at the cardboard underneath her, she explained what the arch was made of. The fabric covering the arch was tied at the back of her head. When she stood up, the ends of the cloth fell to the backs of her knees. She invited me to her place for tea.

Her house, outside the oasis of Palmyra, was on the edge of the desert with other dismal cubes of grey plaster and concrete blocks. Houses I had thought were bunkers were scattered haphazardly on the lower slopes of a barren hill. Um Helif's house had a bit of decoration. Fatima showed me how they had used a comb to plough snaking furrows into the plaster.

It was a three-room house, and in the two rooms I saw, there was only one piece of furniture: a cupboard full of pots and platters. On a shelf built into a concrete wall, mattress pads, blankets, and straw mats were stacked neatly behind a curtain. Gunnysacks were piled on rusty barrels in one corner of the room where Um Helif laid a colourful straw mat on the concrete floor. I could smell the straw and the burlap. The ceiling was the traditional raft of round logs supporting wooden boards; the logs went right through the walls.

Um Helif went into an enclosed courtyard, where the sun

beat on tired plants in faded olive oil tins, to make tea on a gas burner. Fatima and I took off our shoes and sat on the crunchy straw mat. I removed my hat and Helif brought Fatima a comb. I wondered if it had been used on the walls. She knelt beside me and pulled it through my hair. It seemed like a natural thing for her to do and it was undoubtedly necessary. I hadn't known whether I would find a place to stay in Palmyra, so I had only packed essentials, and a hat made a comb unessential. Helif put on my hat and sunglasses. We laughed and called him a tourist.

Um Helif brought in a tray with a tin teapot and three miniature teacups. Squatting barefoot on the concrete floor, she poured steaming tea into tiny cups already carpeted with sugar. One for herself, one for Fatima, and one for me. She gave me the only cup that still had a handle. The tea was strong, and very sweet.

After an easy silence which lasted a few minutes, the hostess set her cup on the floor and, rubbing the sides of her index fingers together, asked whether I was married.

"Yes." If you're going to lie, be consistent.

"Babies?" She had nine—seven girls, two boys—and was shocked that I had none. "*Why?*" she wailed.

I was tempted to say "I'm careful" but instead held one palm up to heaven, shrugged my shoulders and said, "*In shaa' Allah.*" God willing.

How old was I? How long had I been married?

"Two years."

I could see her calculating my fertility odds. "Do you have a problem?" she asked, pointing at my stomach with a look of concern swaddled in pity.

I shrugged again and raised one palm up to heaven.

At her request, Helif brought his mother a framed black and white photograph of a smooth-skinned young man wearing a white *kaffiyah* with a black halo-like cord holding it in place. "My husband," she said, passing her hand over the glass as if to caress his cheek. I had a hard time matching him to the

65

brown wrinkled woman stroking the glass. She had a face like a leather bag tattooed with veins of indigo: a blue star on each cheek; a diamond between her eyes; an X like a hockey stick face-off on her chin; and a chain of circles like blue foam trailing from the corners of her mouth. More tattoos curled around the wrist of her right hand. In the photograph, her husband's face was smooth and clear: his skin untouched by culture, unmarked by time.

What Fatima lacked in tattoos (she had none), she made up for with flashes of gold. I mimed the pain of having a tooth pulled, and she nodded and laughed. Her natural front teeth were flanked by false gold ones. Her mother wore black; Fatima sparkled. Golden leaves adorned the black veil that covered her hair; shiny gold discs were sewn onto the floor-length white velour robe she wore. "She will shine like the sun," said Helif.

Then we didn't say anything for a while. A fly buzzed along the concrete wall above the gunnysacks and barrels. It occurred to me that to the Bedouin, that fly had more meaning than a world of computers, satellites, and software, and I had to agree. The corporate world was far away. After two cups of tea, I gave the family a ballpoint pen, and when Fatima asked, I assured her it was foreign.

◧ *corporate blasphemy*

My other life—before I went to Syria—was corporate reality. Budgets, schedules, meetings, deadlines. The design and development of software to schedule and control the processing of satellite data. A Canadian satellite was going up and the software had to be ready before the launch date. My colleagues and I worked to deadlines, eggs-thrown-at-brick-wall deadlines. I remember thinking that there were billions of people in the world who didn't care one whit about my deadlines—and not just because they didn't know about them. One of my colleagues wore a tie proclaiming: ELEPHANTS DON'T CARE. Unfortunately, I cared. Kind of. Part of me knew the world really didn't need another satellite.

When the work was finished, I stepped off the corporate ladder and went to Syria. My life had been ruled by artificial deadlines for too long. The only *real* deadline is death. I had enough money saved to give myself the gift of time. Sometimes the best thing you can do to your career is ruin it.

But the eternal pleaser left the company on good terms.

"Early retirement," I called it, though I knew my savings wouldn't last for the rest of my life (unless my life were unusually short). I also knew there was a job waiting if I wanted it. The net of security under my freedom. I may have damaged my career, but I didn't ruin it. I've always been too sensible.

✾ after tea

From Palmyra to Damascus was a three-hour bus trip. I settled into a window seat. A heavy-set man boarded the bus. He wore dark trousers, and a short-sleeved red and green plaid shirt. He had a hook nose and his eyebrows came perilously close to meeting. After checking his ticket—seats on the air-conditioned Karnak bus were assigned—the man, who was in his late twenties, sat down somewhere behind me. Only if a bus were full would a ticket seller place a foreign woman beside an Arab woman, or even—God forbid—next to a man. I had two seats to myself and I was looking forward to a peaceful journey through the desert.

But as the bus pulled out of the oasis, the hook-nosed man abandoned the seat that had been assigned to him and came to sit beside me. He spread himself out and his left leg sprawled onto my side of the seat. My legs were crowded against the wall of the bus. Picking up my day pack from the floor, I put it on the seat between us to reclaim a bit of territory without touching him.

The man introduced himself in English. He was a student of veterinary medicine. Was it my imagination or did I catch a whiff of formaldehyde? I pictured the man with his arm deep inside a prolapsing sheep or camel. He had failed many courses and told me veterinarians were not respected in Syria. When he found out I was from Canada, he spoke of a lover—and that's the word he used—whom he had promised to marry. They had planned to emigrate to Montreal. She would go first, and he would follow. But after she had left, he changed his mind. "She phone me many times," he said with a lopsided grin. "She was angry."

He actually grinned. Or was it a smirk? On behalf of myself and every woman who has ever been jilted, I wanted to smack him.

After more chit-chat, which I didn't encourage, he volunteered to tell me a "puzzle" about a "girl *garçon*." There are no waitresses in Syria. Only men work in restaurants.

"A man is in a restaurant. A girl *garçon* say to him, 'You prefer coffee or tea?'" The veterinarian paused for effect and looked at me slyly. "The man say, 'I prefer after tea.'"

I responded with a blank look.

"After tea!" he brayed triumphantly. "The man say, 'I prefer after tea!'"

I ignored him.

"I move this," he said abruptly as he reached for my day pack which was pressed against his leg.

"No, you will not." I held the pack firmly in place. His hand stopped and fell to his thigh like a bird shot in midair. He wiped his palm on his trousers, shrugged, and went back to his puzzle.

" 'I prefer after tea.' You understand?" His lips were thin and he smiled like a snake.

"No."

"Think! Think! After tea. I prefer after tea!"

I thought about it, he repeated his puzzle from beginning to end, and I still didn't understand.

"After tea! I prefer after tea." His voice was oily smooth, his eyes glinted, and his hand rubbed his thigh. He was coiled, ready to strike. "In your alphabet ... after T ... I prefer ... after T." His eyes devoured me.

I looked away and didn't say anything.

"You don't understand." He shook his head and began to explain it again.

"I under*stand*," I interrupted. "I do *not* think it is funny." I spoke loudly and several heads turned to see what the commotion was about.

The man flinched, and his hand balled into a fist, but he didn't say anything. He excused himself and slithered back to his own seat. My day pack filled the empty space beside me and my legs sprawled onto its side of the seat.

◈ *Bludan*

The Desert Festival was the dividing line between cold and hot. In May, Ahmed replaced the portable electric heater I had hovered over through March and most of April with a three-speed electric fan. The days grew warm. I began to hold my breath when I walked past the open garbage bin at the end of the block. To escape the city smells and the heat, I made a day trip to Bludan, where restaurants and limestone villas with red-tile roofs look out at snow-streaked mountains across the border in Lebanon. Huda's family villa was on a side street. She greeted me with kisses on both cheeks and took me by the hand for a tour of the house. Their summer home. You had to cross the courtyard to go from one high-ceilinged room to another. The walls of one bedroom were sprinkled with hand-painted stars.

Family and friends had gathered for Huda's brother's birthday. We sat in the courtyard in the shade of apricot trees. There was beer for the women, *araq* for the men, though I tried a small glass of clear aniseed firewater. Huda's sister-in-law, Laila, a beautiful dark-haired woman, danced solo to copper-tinted music. Her clothes were western—a red tank top and tailored khaki shorts—yet her dance was an Arabian enchantment of smouldering incense and hammered brass. No wonder they lock up their women, I thought. The eroticism was palpable. Our hands kept time and we cheered her on until the music ended and she sat down on a bench beside her husband, who handed her a beer. Huda turned the cassette over and motioned for me to dance. Part of me wanted to let go the reins, run free, but the rest of me would have needed more *araq*. Though I've always wished I could live my life with the unselfconscious grace and passion that dancers seem to possess, instead of unleashing an erotic storm, I bummed a cigarette and pulled smoke into my lungs.

We feasted on *tabbouleh* (cracked wheat, tomatoes, parsley, green onions, olive oil, and lemon juice), and *kebab, kebab, kebab*—skewers of chicken, mutton, and beef grilled over wood charcoals. We ate with our hands. Lettuce leaves scooped up *tabbouleh*, and flat round bread clutched hot and spicy *kebab*. I ate and ate and ate and ate—slowly, slowly—because the only way to refuse more food was to be in the process of eating.

The birthday cake was chocolate with white icing and pink roses. Huda's brother blew out the candles, then held a knife three feet above the cake and let it drop. The men circled around him, rhythmically clapping and chanting. An Arabic version of "Happy Birthday"? Huda translated: "It was a dark day when you were born." The cake was moist and sweet.

That evening wispy clouds took on delicate hues of pinks and greys like the colours on the roof of a painter's mouth. The sun sank into Lebanon, leaving an ephemeral ribbon of silver light etched on the mountain horizon. I felt at peace with the earth, with humanity, with life. Why couldn't that feeling last? It never does—for me, anyway. On the way back to Damascus, a statue of President Assad caught in mid-stride waved from the top of a hill.

▣ *something funny*

To visit the Golan Heights, one must first go to the U.N. office in Damascus to obtain a special permit. The office was about a block and a half from my house, but I had trouble finding it because the building was unmarked. I asked a man unloading boxes of paper from the trunk of a car if he knew where it was. He didn't, and after nervously looking right, then left, added in English, "This is a dangerous area. You must not take pictures, you must not ask questions. I advise you to leave." There was something funny about the neighbourhood I lived in.

Meecro drivers wouldn't let me out on the street below my house. They drove on, ignoring my request, or questioning me with "Here? Here?" until we were past where I had wanted to get out. My Arabic was poor, yet it was odd that drivers could understand me in other parts of the city—including one block west or two blocks east of that particular stretch. One day, instead of being polite, I simply shouted "*Qeif!*" Stop! The *meecro* screeched to a halt. I slid the van door open and scrambled out. I had done it! I had finally gotten a *meecro* to stop at the closest point to my house. The driver and the other passengers looked so dumbfounded I almost laughed. Arabic coming out of a foreigner's mouth always seemed to surprise people. But suddenly—my feet had barely touched the pavement, I hadn't even closed the door—a sharp whistle cracked the air. A whistle that demanded attention—and got it. The driver and the passengers looked behind me, and the sudden tension in their faces took the pleasure out of my victory. I turned to see what they were gaping at: a soldier running towards me with a bayonet. My eyes focussed on the blade. My hands went up, an instinctive reaction. The soldier shouted at the driver. Arabic had never sounded so dangerous. "I live here, I live here." How many times did I say that? The driver and passengers all spoke together, waving their hands in my direction and babbling things I couldn't decipher. But I understood they blamed me—I felt like the bad kid who gets the whole class into trouble—and they disowned me. The soldier slashed the air with his bayonet to wave the *meecro* on. The door slid shut and the van sped off without me. The soldier's anthracite eyes scanned the street. "I live here, I live here." It seemed so ridiculous. How could a woman in a skirt, a cotton blouse, and sandals be such a threat? A grunt and a flick of his bayonet informed me that I could go home unharmed. There was definitely something funny about the neighbourhood I lived in.

The first time I walked on the street below my house, a tall man wearing a black suit stood on the corner by the mosque as if waiting for a date. To avoid eye contact, which might be construed as flirting, I looked past him, off into the distance. He stared at me and continued to stare—long and hard; I could feel his eyes on my face. Finally, when I came close, I lowered my head, using my hat brim to block his view of my face—and I looked straight down at a machine gun. I hoped he wasn't waiting for a date.

There was always a man in a black suit with a machine gun standing on that corner. Two more blocked the entrance of a nearby street, and a dozen waited at the other end of the forbidden street in a gathering place for long black cars with tinted windows and multiple aerials. Some of the men carried walkie-talkies and revolvers. I learned to let them examine my face, because if I hid behind my hat brim too soon, they stopped me and wanted to know where I was going.

Throughout Damascus, soldiers with bayonets and machine guns drink tea and hiss at foreign women while guarding crucial intersections, government buildings, and embassies. I ignored hissing (a low grade form of flirtation) and obeyed sharp, attention-getting whistles which meant: whatever you're doing, stop it. If you're moving, either stop or move in a different direction. If you're stopped, start moving.

Soldiers were everywhere. Men in black suits weren't. And unlike the soldiers, many of whom were doing compulsory military service, the men in black suits were always alert.

I asked Ahmed about the men in black suits and the machine guns. President Assad sometimes holds important meetings in a nearby building, he said. Did he believe that? Maybe. I didn't. I knew what security for President Assad was like because on the first day of the *Eid al-Adha* religious festival he had prayed at al-Rawda Mosque a few blocks south of my house. I got up early, hoping to catch a glimpse of him going into the mosque, but president-watching was not encouraged. Busloads of police, soldiers, and men in black suits arrived long before he did, and I couldn't get anywhere near the mosque. I went home and watched Assad pray on television.

Much later, after I had moved on, I read about the dark side of the Assad regime—beatings, torture, imprisonment without trial, prisoners machine-gunned in their cells—and I learned that there was an interrogation centre somewhere in the vicinity of my little house in Damascus.

Not very funny. Not funny at all.

⊞ expatriate scandal

British accents. Muffled voices. Whispers. The wives of Shell Oil workers gossiping at the American Library Club in Damascus. The children are ensconced in boarding schools in England. And the husbands? The hiss of a woman's horror. Through paperback stacks of mystery, romance, and adventure, I heard a stage whisper, "Didn't you hear? Her husband's run off with a belly dancer!" The fragrance of sensuous full-blown roses crept in through an open door.

✦ laundry

The previous tenant of the little house in Damascus had laundry service: Offa washed his clothes for him. She had no intention of continuing the service for a woman. Before I moved in, Ahmed installed a miniature balcony with half a dozen metre-long clotheslines outside the kitchen window. He called it a *balkone*, stressing the second syllable. Shortly after I moved in, he bought a washing machine for the house. "Small, small," he said several times, trying to manage my expectations. Still I wasn't quite prepared for my Syrian washing machine. It was the evolutionary step between a washboard and a wringer washer: it did the washing; I did the wringing.

My washing machine was a pale blue plastic bucket with a drain plug in the bottom. In the side of the bucket was a slot for a moulded fan run by an electric motor. Water, detergent, and dirty clothes went into the bucket, and, at the flip of a switch, the fan would slosh the water around, creating suds, and thereby washing the clothes. At least that was the theory.

In reality, when I flipped the switch, more often than not,

nothing happened. The fan didn't turn; the water didn't slosh; there were no suds. A whiny hum assured me that the machine was plugged in, that it was getting power. However, the fan wouldn't move until I had stuck my arm into the hot water, pushing soiled laundry aside, and nervously placed my fingers on one of its flared plastic wings. After I had done a few spins with the fan, it would fly past my fingers to continue on alone—sloshing water, creating suds, and washing clothes.

The first time I used the machine, I thought the water level line, marked in black about two inches below the top of the bucket, was a maximum, not a necessity. If the water level was too low, the fan would fling the water out of the bucket, all around the room. After that I did laundry in the shower stall.

The Syrian washing machine made me realize how disconnected I had become from dirt. When you wash clothes in an automatic machine, you don't see the dirt—it disappears with the water down an unseen drain. With my machine I could watch my clothes turn a pool of clear water into a mud puddle.

After washing the clothes, I rinsed the soap out in the bathroom sink and wrung them as well as I could by hand, before hanging them out to dry. Wet laundry shared the *balkone* with doves doing high-wire acts on the clotheslines. My landlady Offa was freed from taking in laundry for her tenants. Water dripped on the courtyard soccer field of little boys three storeys below.

◼ *my godmother*

Srouran came to my house in Damascus for English lessons. He was a big heavy man in his early twenties who had taken lessons from the former tenant of the house and continued taking them from me. He told me he sold women's shoes in his father's store in the *Souq al-Hamidiyyah*, the main covered market, and he said he wanted to improve his English for business reasons. He didn't own a car, yet I once saw him drive up in a big fat Mercedes with tinted glass.

Srouran asked for a discount for his English lessons, saying he was saving money to get married. He didn't have a fiancée. He warned me not to hike up the mountain, Jebel Qassioun, alone. He said it was dangerous, yet everyone else said it was safe. And with a rude reminder that I was much closer to menopause than puberty, he rebuked me for not having had children yet: "You must hurry! You are *not* young."

Srouran was not my favourite student.

One day he saw a postcard of the gigantic Omayyed Mosque in the Old City lying on my table. After his last lesson, when he had reprimanded me for not having seen the ancient mosque, which happens to house a mausoleum for John the Baptist's head, I had made a point of visiting it.

"You are sending the postcard to your husband?" he asked me.

"No, I'm sending it to my godparents."

"Godparents!?" He looked startled.

I explained that when I was born, my parents chose a man and a woman to be my godparents. If anything happened to my parents and they couldn't look after me, then my godmother and godfather would take care of me and ensure that I was raised as a Christian.

Srouran shook his head in disbelief.

"Where is your godmother?" he demanded to know.

"In Canada. She lives with her husband, my godfather, across the river from my parents." With my finger rippling the tablecloth, I drew the North Fork of the Oldman River as it flows out of the Rockies and into the foothills of Alberta. I pointed out the homesteads on either side of the river. Srouran blinked his eyes and shook his head as if he had seen a ghost.

"Your godmother, is she eating? Sleeping?"

"Yes. She eats, she sleeps."

"She eats! She sleeps!" He looked at me incredulously.

"Yes. She even gardens."

Srouran pulled a silver cigarette case out of his shirt pocket and lit up a Marlboro, fumbling with his gold lighter. Hiding behind a curtain of smoke, he continued his interrogation.

"Your mother, does she have a godmother?"

I nodded and added, "But I think she's dead now."

"Is she eating? Sleeping?"

"Not now. She's dead. But she used to eat and sleep."

Srouran was not happy. Over and over he grilled me about whether my godmother and the godmothers of my maternal ancestors ate and slept. Finally his shock and disbelief turned to anger and righteousness. After crushing his cigarette in the ashtray, he took a deep breath and shuddered. Then he lectured me in a voice powered by emotion.

"There is no God but God, and Mohammed is the Prophet of God." He had recited the core creed of Islam. "For Muslims there is only *one* God. For you, there are three! God, godfather, godmother." A finger lashed out of his meaty fist for each of what he thought were my gods. I half expected a bolt of lightning and a clap of thunder to accompany each one.

"No, no, no. Christians have only one God," I hastened to reassure him. "It's the same God as your God. There is only one God. Godmother, godfather—they are not gods."

"They are not gods?"

"No. Absolutely not. They are people just like you and me. They're nice people but they are not gods. 'Godmother' and 'godfather' are just names."

"Why this name?" he demanded.

I put my hands up in the air. "I don't know. It's English. It's just a name."

After he left, I wondered what he would think of Hinduism or other polytheistic religions. It occurred to me later that the thought of a deity being female had upset him the most. We never discussed it, though, because Srouran was suddenly very busy. I didn't see him for a couple of months, and when I did, I wished I hadn't. The money he owed me wasn't worth collecting. But more about that later.

I don't know what happened to Srouran, but my godmother is still eating and sleeping. She even gardens.

◈ *survival*

On an overhead walkway near the telephone office in Damascus, shopkeepers sell socks and undershirts out of cardboard boxes piled on the rough metal floor. At the top of the stairs, a woman in a dark blue raincoat sat on a dirty scrap of cardboard. A black cloth hid her face and hair. A coarse blanket covered two children beside her. A baby was on her lap. The woman cradled the baby with one hand, and with the other, she begged. Her voice shot through the grating roar of trucks on the street below. I couldn't understand what she was saying, yet I went out of my way to use the walkway, just so I could give her a bit of money.

Sometimes a man sat on the sidewalk in front of the post office, near the men selling lottery tickets. The man's body was a geometric line drawing. His bones were scalpels threatening to cut their way out of his skin. With his bare knees drawn up to his chin, he looked like a brittle-legged spider. How could he walk on those crisp, snappable, spider-like limbs? A daddy-longlegs. I wanted to step on him, squash him into the sidewalk.

I never saw the man come or go. I imagined him being carried away in a basket, his bones dismantled—socket by socket—into a chaotic heap like pieces of tangled straw. But I only ever saw him sitting on the sidewalk near the lottery tickets, below a larger-than-life painted banner of the Syrian president draped across the front of the post office. The emaciated man sat quietly, a silent reminder to everyone who passed that life itself is a lottery and he had not had much luck. A faded yellow cloth was spread out in front of him to collect spare change thrown his way.

I intended to give the man money, yet whenever I saw him, which wasn't often, I shuddered and drew away. He repelled me, annoyed me. Why didn't he just eat, gain some weight, get back on his feet? As if he were to blame. I passed him and his jaundiced cloth with my fingers clamped on an unopened wallet. With a guilt-singed conscience, I made my way to the overhead walkway. I told myself that the woman in the dark blue raincoat, the woman with children to feed, the woman whose face I had never seen, needed my money more.

✦ *in the hands of God*

When it came to crossing busy streets in Damascus, I was like a child: I tried not to do it alone. I shadowed the locals, putting my life into the hands of unsuspecting strangers. Preferably older strangers because teenage boys have no fear of death.

On my way to the *souq* one day to change money, I latched onto a lumpy old woman with liver-spotted hands. We were partway across a wide street when a chaotic surge of busses and trucks and cars surrounded us. An urban stampede of bumpers, metal, exhaust fumes, horns, rubber tires. A green truck bore down on us. The trumpeting blare of an elephant horn. A feather duster swaddled in a glittery scarf adorned the hood. The lumpy old woman was beside me. We didn't move. The truck would hit her first. Perhaps her generous hips would break the axle, bringing the vehicle to a grinding halt before it hit me. At the last second the truck veered, passing so close I could smell the metal, and the draught pulled at my skirt. Behind the truck was a battered, pale yellow taxi with a bunch of plastic grapes hanging from the rear-view mirror. A white baby shoe with a side-buckle clasp dangled from the bumper. *Beep! Beep!* The woman and I were frozen, petrified. Live statues. Sculptures in the middle of a busy street. Vehicle after vehicle—trucks, taxis, busses, cars, cars, and more cars—swerved around us. Horns, diesel, exhaust fumes, chaos. Drivers didn't bother with lanes.

The woman and I didn't move. I wondered how well she could see. Her eyes were hidden behind a black veil. In fact, her whole face was hidden behind a black veil. And from under the veil, through the cacophony of motors and horns, I heard a muffled "*In shaa' Allah!*" God willing!

I looked at her in horror. "Bloody hell!" I muttered. I had entrusted her with my life—I thought she knew what she was doing!

Then the woman moved forward. I stuck with her. It was better than being left out there alone. Intoning *in shaa' Allah*, the old woman forged ahead, slowly but surely, parting the waters of a turbulent metal sea.

We reached the shore safely and the old woman waddled off into the bustling shadows of the *souq* as if nothing unusual had happened. I stood on the foot-high curb, feeling nauseous. My eyes were watering, my knees felt weak, and I was shaking. A crest-shaped sign on Said al-Jabri Avenue announces the previous year's scores for traffic accidents, including pedestrians wounded, pedestrians killed. I had almost become a scoreboard statistic. What a horrible way to die. I took a deep breath. The aroma of fresh bread came from a nearby cart. It was a relief to enter the pedestrian-only, shadowy confines of the *souq*. Along with relief came the realization that the old woman had known exactly what she was doing: crossing the street in Damascus is a matter of faith.

▦ *I wish*

One evening I saw a boy, maybe five years old, or a stunted seven, sitting cross-legged at the edge of a busy sidewalk. His shoulders were hunched and he fanned himself with a wad of crumpled bills. He looked bored. Directly in front of the boy, towering above him, a man with a bushy moustache looked down at the display on the scales under his feet. Was the man putting on weight? Or losing it? The boy didn't care—as long as the man had paid. He was just another customer for a working boy in Damascus.

One morning on an overhead walkway, the safest way to cross the street, an older boy in blue jeans and a mustard sweatshirt greeted me with an excited "*Madame!*" and smiled so engagingly, I couldn't refuse. For one lire, I stood on his grimy bathroom scales and watched red and black numbers whiz by, then rock back and forth before settling into place. According to the scales, I weighed more than I had ever weighed in my entire life. It wasn't true. A village woman looking at a picture taken shortly before I left Canada had admonished me with

"You were fat, now you're skinny. You must eat!" My clothes were hanging on me.

The boy was happy to pose for a photograph. Oval face, ruddy cheeks, right hand on the walkway railing, left hand on his hip, right foot resting on the stone block he had been sitting on, pink and white scales at his feet. He didn't ask for anything in return, but I gave him five lire and he seemed pleased.

The walkway was L-shaped, and just around the corner was another boy with scales. He didn't greet me with an engaging smile or an excited "*Madame!*" His eyes didn't twinkle, they were dull. His clothes were shabby and one or two sizes too small. The boy looked glum, almost sullen. Hopeless. I walked past him thinking he should really take a marketing lesson from the child around the corner. Traces of the ammonia stench of urine fouled the stairway leading back down to the street.

Shame, shame, I thought later. Children who aren't blessed with winning smiles deserve better. The ones who don't reach out to demand kindness and attention need it the most.

I wish, I wish, I wish, I wish.

I wish I had weighed myself again.

I wish I had taken his picture.

I wish I had given him a hundred lire.

I wish I had given that boy a reason—a chance—to smile.

ululations

Howl. Jagged wail. High-pitched scribble on an oscillating canvas. Grief or joy. Shards of silence stuck in a scream. How to describe ululations? The first time I heard them, I was in Egypt, camped on the west bank of the Nile, dancing around a fire. There was an eclipse of the full moon, and a felucca captain, the Nubian, Abdullah. Wood smoke, ochre flames, brown face under a pale blue turban, throat cocked to ululate: vocal fireworks, lava flow ejaculation; aural dilation.

Why was it that I wanted to learn? I don't know any more. It sounded like fun. Idle speculation. A twenty-five-cent wager made in a ranchhouse in Alberta that I could do it by the end of the year. The years rolled by—double or nothing—with a gambling debt carried forward ... until I went to Syria (and spent thousands of dollars!) for the sake of a two-dollar bet.

Mutton burgers with melted cheese. French fries cooked on the balcony. Flat round bread: scoop for chickpea *hummus*; wrap for deep-fried cauliflower squirted with lemon. Lunch with Offa in the sunroom of her apartment in Mezze, a modern suburb of Damascus. Knife peeling a red tongue from an apple. Apricot juice, ice cold. "Offa, can you teach me to ululate?" I yelped like a yappy dog to demonstrate. A waterfall of laughter, then Offa cupped her hand over her mouth for a ring of sound, the wind, a wave, the desert rushing in. "Yes! *How?* How did you do that?" Her hand dropped, her tongue flickered. An open-mouthed demonstration. Within a few minutes my own voice was rising through hoops of Offa's laughter. I did it! We did it! Exaltation! Offa taught me how to fling my voice into the heavens, to wait with an open throat for the moment of purity when angels descend and the gods decree a celebration of silence. The feathers of angels. Ululations and silence.

"Why you want to learn?" Offa was excited. There was laughter in her eyes.

I had won a bet. A two-dollar bet. A big one for me. I rarely risk more than a nickel or a quarter. Few things are more satisfying than winning a trivial bet. But I was afraid Offa wouldn't understand my joy.

Egypt. Five years earlier. A beach house outside Alexandria. A lucky streak in a dice game. I raked in coins and cigarettes. At the end of the night, after the early morning call to the mosque had sounded, Samir, who had lost again and again, rose to go. Ashraf dipped into my loot to give Samir the coins and most of the cigarettes (I had already smoked a few) he had lost. "Is he so poor?" I asked when his car pulled out of the driveway. And Ashraf, who had me buy beer for him during the holy month of Ramadan, replied sternly, "Islam forbids gambling."

So I grinned at Offa and said, "It's fun." I could hardly wait to tell my sister.

◼ *watercolour days*

I settled into a routine. Arabic lessons every other day generated between three to five hours' worth of homework. The rest of my time was free. Day after day after week after week. Time stretched out. The world slowed down. I was never in a hurry. And I was never bored. The days ran together like watercolours on paper scrolls. Ahmed helped me at the Immigration Office by making up plausible excuses for why I needed another scroll. The American Language Center was always looking for English teachers and a job there would have given me a residence permit (as well as money to eat out), doing away with my tourist scrolls, which dwindled in size from four weeks to two weeks to ten days and so on. But I wasn't ready to give up my freedom.

I tutored English privately but I didn't enjoy it. I had two students. One was a playboy type who wanted to improve his English so he could talk with his Russian girlfriend. He struck me as the kind of guy who would piss in a woman's beer and let her drink it for a joke. I was glad when he disappeared after two lessons. The other fellow didn't last much longer, and although the money would have helped, I was glad to be rid of them both. I didn't want my mind harnessed as a workhorse pulling a plough for English furrows.

I was busy planting Arabic seeds. I learned the words I needed for my explorations: *khaeema* (tent), *jaami'* or *masjid* (mosque), *qadees* (saint), *maqbara* (graveyard), *maqaam* (mausoleum). My favourite was *sunoonoo*, a word that captures the heart of its namesake, the swallow, embroidering the Damascus sky.

I normally avoid television, but in Syria sometimes I watched the news in French and Arabic and then finally in English to figure out what had happened. Sprinkled throughout the Arabic version was a guttural *fuck it*. My dictionary enlightened me that *faqat* means 'only'.

I never did learn the word for 'breakfast', possibly because it's easy to mime eating, but the more likely reason is that—I know this is blasphemy for some people—with the exception of sweets, food doesn't mean that much to me. I eat to stay alive; I don't live to eat. If it weren't for packaged foods and multivitamins, I suspect rickets or scurvy would have finished me off long ago. Unfortunately, I couldn't find packaged foods in Damascus and my budget didn't allow me to eat out in the kinds of places that wouldn't cause chronic dysentery.

Offa showed me the "clean" shops in my neighbourhood. To get to them, I had to walk past a bakery where flat round bread lay stretched out on the sidewalk or draped over the iron spikes of a rail fence to cool, past cubbyhole grocery stores, past stationary shops, a tailor shop, past floral displays mounted on easel-like sticks, past a pastry shop and a white marble mosque, and past a roadside trough for donkeys. Then the gnarled fingers of an old man in a crocheted skullcap plopped buns into a bag as his toothless gums blessed each one with a number: *wahed, itneen, talataa, arba'a.*

At the "clean" pastry shop, I stocked up on chocolate croissants, strawberry tarts, and rice pudding. I tried the croissants at a pastry shop Offa hadn't rated as "clean" and they weren't nearly as good.

The "clean" grocery store had a neon sign and a cash register instead of a plastic bucket full of crumpled bills. It also had a cooler full of cheese wedges, boxed milk from Denmark, and Syrian butter, which was cheaper than margarine. But I didn't feel right about shopping at the most prosperous store in the neighbourhood, so I strayed regularly, buying cans and jars and noodles in the cubbyhole shops that didn't have neon signs or coolers. The owner of a toiletries blanket-shop spread out on the sidewalk earned my gratitude and loyalty by pointing out that the toothpaste I had in my hand was shaving cream.

To prepare hot meals in the small house, I slid open the kitchen window, raised the white enamel stove cover, then, swallowing fear (I've never been fond of gas), gave the valve on a blue canister a counterclockwise crank, turned a knob on the front panel, and flicked a spark-making wand over hissing gas until flaming tongues sprang out of the burner. After cooking (I use the word loosely), I turned off the gas and shut the window before sitting down to dinner. My first hot meal was gummy strands of stringy cheese on boiled macaroni.

I tried boiling fresh vegetables with the macaroni to make the dish slightly less repulsive. Cauliflower, carrots, peas. My mother wrote that the garden of an elderly neighbour had gone unplanted for the first time ever, so she had taken a pail of peas over to the old woman, saying, "You couldn't let a summer go by without shelling peas." I wrote home to say the first batch of peas I shelled, after carefully selecting firm pods in a cubbyhole shop in Damascus, turned out to be broad beans (the vegetable centrefold page in my Arabic-English dictionary made identification possible); and that after rejecting miniature tins of tomato paste in favour of a half litre jar of *thickened tomato guice*, hoping it might be spaghetti sauce, I found myself with more tomato paste in the fridge than I had used in the previous decade.

Luckily, Offa was a good cook and she invited me to eat

97

with them often. I was only disappointed once. In the morning she phoned and invited me to eat with them that afternoon. She was always reluctant to specify a time but she promised to call later when Ahmed was on his way to pick me up. After accepting the invitation, I recalled that the playboy had a one-hour English lesson scheduled for two o'clock. I didn't think it would interfere with the invitation but I called Offa back to tell her.

"*Malesh,*" she said. Never mind.

Ahmed dropped off a small jar of Nescafé coffee around noon. My student arrived at two o'clock and left just after three. Then I reviewed Arabic vocabulary while waiting for a phone call from Offa. My stomach began to complain. I finished a packet of cookies, then picked up the phone to check for a dial tone. I tried to read. The afternoon wore on. I checked the phone again. I thought about calling Offa, but was afraid it might be rude. My stomach nagged me into eating an apple. Afternoon wore into evening. I turned on the television and watched young boys spin drums full of lottery tickets. I switched channels. A wide-eyed, long-haired woman smiled as she sang the praises of chocolate biscuits to the tune of "When the Saints Go Marching In." Then Dr. David Suzuki came on, apparently speaking fluent Arabic. I switched off the television and wrote in my journal:

"Come eat with us." I'm starving! Have they forgotten me? Did I misunderstand? I hate this drab waiting. I'm pinned to the house like a moth on a Styrofoam board. And when they call I shall act as if I've spent my time in meaningful pursuits and just happened to free up when the phone rang. The clock snickers, its hands cover its wicked mouth. If they simply forgot, will they later remember and offer overblown flowery apologies? To which I am supposed to graciously reply, "Malesh. No problem. Yes, of course I ate something." Or will they say nothing and whatever happened will remain one of life's little mysteries? My stomach shouts. I hate waiting for the phone to ring. But at least this time I'm not waiting for a man.

My cupboards were bare. Because of the invitation I hadn't bothered to shop for groceries. I had no bread, no vegetables, and only a few noodles in the house. Eventually I ate, alone in the kitchen, with my feet up on the windowsill. Supper was *thickened tomato guice* smeared on twenty-seven pathetic little cockleshell noodles. I counted them.

The next morning, on my way home from the "clean" pastry shop, it occurred to me that Offa probably thought I had cancelled because of the English lesson.

Not long after that I received a parcel card in the mail. The woman at the Poste Restante wicket told me when and where I could pick up the parcel. A care package from Canada! A surprise shipment of Kraft Dinner and other culinary delights. I'm not kidding when I say the parcel brought tears of joy to my eyes. My mother had greatly enhanced my chances for survival.

I was a regular at the Poste Restante wicket in the main post office on Said al-Jabri Avenue. My favourite clerk was the woman who gave me the parcel card. She was in her forties, a handsome woman with good bones. A cream-coloured scarf covered her hair, and she wore a fan-shaped dress coat buttoned up to her chin, the fashionable way to meet the Islamic dress code. She remembered my name and by the time I reached the front of the line, she always had my letters set aside for me.

Sometimes a younger woman worked at the counter. She held the bundle of Poste Restante letters up close to her chest like a poker player. Occasionally she would pause (and pretend) to compare the name on an envelope with the block letter name I had given her. She wouldn't show me the envelope, and I didn't believe she could read the Roman alphabet. Not once—NOT ONCE—did I receive a letter when the poker player was on duty.

When she had finished with the bundle of letters, I would smile and thank her, and sometimes add, "Tomorrow, *in shaa' Allah*," hoping that, God willing, *she* wouldn't be there. I didn't like her. She wasn't the least bit friendly, and her coldness made me wonder if she considered the nakedness of my uncovered hair and partially exposed collarbone obscene. I couldn't even get a smile out of her, yet I was careful to remain polite. You should never antagonize a person who controls your mail— even if you're convinced she can't read.

A sharp-faced man with stiff white whiskers was the opposite of the poker player. He tossed every letter that wasn't addressed in Arabic down on the counter and let me choose which ones I wanted to take home. I hoped there weren't any foreigners collecting Canadian stamps in the city.

The Poste Restante wicket was often the first indication I had that a holiday had sneaked up on me. Mother's Day, Martyrs Day (the news showed President Assad dining with the children of martyrs), Evacuation Day (marks the beginning of Syrian independence when France withdrew), Easter, Orthodox Easter. The list went on. In my next life, I thought, I want to come back as a clerk at the Poste Restante counter in Damascus. The post office was open. I could buy stamps and mail letters, but the Poste Restante wicket was closed.

Eid al-Adha didn't sneak up on me though. The holiday begins on the last day of the pilgrimage to Mecca, and Huda told me on Tuesday that it would start on Wednesday and last until Saturday. I was at the post office when *Eid al-Adha* started with a *boom*. A postcard seller told me twenty-one booms marked the beginning of the holiday. I walked to where I could see the sky sizzle so bright my eyes flinched. My body recoiled at each *boom*. Smoke rolled and curled and thinned to a net, and gradually disappeared. *Eid al-Adha* had begun. But I didn't yet know what that meant.

The next day I saw eighty head of sheep quivering in a corner. Men dragged live rams across the pavement; dead rams lay on the curb. Butcher hooks hung from eucalyptus trees, and puddles of blood brightened the white marble steps of a mosque on Nazhem Pasha Street. I looked up *Adha* in my dictionary: sacrifice. *Eid al-Adha* is the Festival of the Sacrifice which celebrates Abraham's willingness to kill his own son (Ishmael, according to Muslim belief, not Isaac) for Allah, and the Angel Gabriel bringing a ram to take his place at the last moment. In any case, the first day of *Eid al-Adha* is a sad day for sheep. I called it Bloody Wednesday.

Besides slaughtering sheep on the first day of the holiday, Syrians visit their dead. By chance, that was the day I visited the Martyrs Graveyard at Nazhha on the outskirts of Damascus. Row upon row of identical graves. Dandelion globes were seeds of life amidst the dead. Over a thousand men—young men— martyred, and there was room for plenty more. Stacks of blank tombstones waited in the wings. Children, bright splashes of colour and energy, ran into the graveyard. Adults followed more slowly. A woman in black rocked and cried by the grave of a twenty-year-old man who had been dead for thirteen years. A boy carried a palm leaf. His t-shirt read: *We are coming.*

Yes, of course.

We are coming.

One day in the *souq*, a hairband merchant took me up on the roof. We passed from the bustling shadow world of the *souq* into sunlit peace and calm with Jebel Qassioun on my left and the minarets of the Omayyed Mosque on my right. Electrical wires crisscrossing the roof were snakes dropping into ventilation holes. The merchant broke off a piece of an ancient beam in a fragmented wall and urged me to do the same. The wood turned to dust in our fingers.

The days stretched out. Scrolls unfurled. The colours stayed wet. Time expanded. Interlude in Damascus. *We are coming.* Wood and flesh disappear. An Arab boy carried a palm leaf to a grave. We are all coming, every last one of us, but I wasn't in a hurry to turn into dust. I was able to live in slow motion.

part two
Syrian sorties

◈ travels with a man

When I was in my early twenties, I set off on a journey around the world. It was my first trip outside North America and various well-meaning people told me it wasn't safe for a woman—although they probably said "girl"—to travel alone. My mother warned me not to talk to strangers; I asked her how I would order food.

I travelled to Japan and across what was then the Soviet Union under the protective wing of a tour group consisting largely of left-wing senior citizens who had, oddly enough, profited well from capitalism. I disliked the discipline and the timetables: the very things that allow an organized tour to run smoothly. When our train arrived in Helsinki, I was relieved to strike out on my own.

In my solo travels, I encountered another set of well-meaning people who informed me that it wasn't safe for a woman to be travelling alone. Since I was travelling by myself, and intended to continue doing so, one could hardly tell me with any credibility that it wasn't safe in the country I was in or in any of the countries I had already visited. I noticed that the dangerous-country-for-a-woman-travelling-alone was always just over the horizon—some place where I had not yet been and could, therefore, not refute the wisdom of my current well-wisher, sitting with his wife tucked neatly under his arm.

And when I had reached that "dangerous" country, without being raped at the border, drugged in my hotel room, enslaved in a harem, or imprisoned in a brothel, I would come across another well-wisher with the sage advice that I had best hook up with a man before continuing on to the next country, just over the horizon. It seemed to be common knowledge that it would be safer for me, and certainly easier, to travel with a man.

After I had been in Syria for two and a half months, my partner, Gerd, joined me for a month's holiday. I became the female half of a heterosexual couple and suddenly no one (other than Gerd, of course) would talk to me.

When I asked a man something in Arabic, he would answer looking directly at Gerd, who couldn't understand a word. My questions were answered without so much as a nod in my direction. The same thing happened in English. It would have been disrespectful for an Arab man to look at another man's "wife" right under his nose, but still, I found it unnerving. I felt like an invisible force. When I was alone, Arab men spoke to *me*. I existed.

On the Mediterranean coast, Gerd and I tracked down the caretaker of some beach chalets for rent. The man was in his early thirties and spoke no English. I told him we wanted to look at the chalets, and the man offered Gerd a key and asked him for money. I translated for Gerd and then told the man we wanted to look inside the chalets before paying. Again he told Gerd how much a chalet was and asked him for money. Using every variation of Arabic grammar I knew, I told him again and again and again that we wanted to look at the places first. Eventually he agreed.

The chalets were spread out and we drove to each one with me crammed into the back seat of our rental car, a Volkswagen Beetle, with the backpacks. The caretaker sat in the front with Gerd, who was driving that day. At the chalets the men got out and, as I was pushing the bucket seat forward so I could get out too, the caretaker shut the door. We drove to three chalets and three times he shut the car door. Surely Gerd could decide on a chalet alone! Three times I leaned over the seat and let myself out, remembering that in Arabic "you want" addressed to a man sounds exactly like "she wants." Together we decided to rent elsewhere, mostly because the chalets were dingy.

When I travelled alone, Syrian women approached me, invited me into their homes. We talked and sang, drank tea, and laughed. With a man at my side, the world of women was closed to me. In Raqqa, two friendly young women gave us wonderfully accurate directions to a hotel that turned out to be a brothel, but other women shied away from Gerd and me. I understood it was impossible for an unrelated man to enter into their world, but still I felt like an outcast. I missed the company of women.

In my travels with a man in Syria, I found that I didn't exist in the male world, except to be stared at from a distance, and I couldn't gain access to the female. I felt isolated, alone. A well-wisher might point out that I wasn't alone, I had the company of a man, and that in any case, isolation is a very small price to pay for personal safety. I don't think I'm reckless and I would never call myself brave, because really, at home or abroad, with or without an army of men, no matter the price you've paid, safety is always an illusion.

▣ *expectations*

The gas gauge was on empty. Gerd and I drove past garages displaying tires and cans of oil, but there were no pumps. "There'll be gas in Ras al-Bassit. It's a resort. They have to sell gas." I was sure of it. Reason is a fine thing. It's like mortar for worries: trowel it on thick and the cracks in your logic disappear. The road wound through the green mountains along the Syrian coast before emerging at the Mediterranean, not far from the Turkish border. Lavender hollyhocks frilled the ditches.

Ras al-Bassit was much smaller than we had expected. The main street was a dirt road. On the west side of it, hunched under dusty palms, the flat-roofed grubby faces of chalets gaped at the Mediterranean, where the bare flesh of men and boys in swimming trunks mocked the sodden, long-sleeved, full-length robes of women and girls sitting in the surf fully dressed. On the other side of the road, in the grocery store, a few tins stood like exclamation points punctuating bare shelves. After inspecting some beach chalets, we took a room in the only hotel, a high-rise promising to snare gentle breezes. The restaurant, the only one that was open, served chicken and French fries and litre bottles of al-Charq beer on a terrace by the black pebble beach. The whole town smelled like the sea.

But there were no pumps. We had reached our destination with the gas gauge sitting on empty—and there were no pumps. We didn't have enough gas to leave.

In desperation I leaned out the window of our rented VW Beetle and called out to a man dabbing blue paint on a sign. *Benzeen?* He waved his brush at a tire shop, one with cans of oil. An elderly couple emerged from the shadows, brandishing a funnel and a jerry can. *Benzeen! Benzeen!* It seemed that customers were rare. For them and for us, it was as if they were offering champagne. We established the price. Then the old woman held the funnel in the mouth of the gas tank while her husband poured. I gave their grandson a pen and a rubber spider my nephews had given me. Gasoline fumes made us giddy. We ignored the petrol that ran down the side of the car, just like we had ignored all the gas stations featuring tires and cans of oil on the road to Ras al-Bassit. As always, layers of gauze, cataracts of perception, covered our eyes. We can only see the things we are looking for.

✦ *whirlwind tour*

Two days after Gerd arrived, he hiked to the top of Jebel Qassioun alone, past the point where civilians are supposed to stop, and nearly landed in prison. The soldiers who held him hadn't seen him taking a souvenir photograph of their military compound, otherwise he might not have been able to get up and walk out of the commander's office with an abrupt *I'm leaving,* and hike back down the mountain the way he did.

Gerd didn't like Damascus. Driving in from the airport late at night, his first impression had been a hesitant *dirty, grey.* The next day he added *chaotic, noisy* and, after the incident on the mountain, *dangerous.* Too many soldiers, too many machine guns for a German-Canadian who can't stand uniformed authority.

We travelled to Jordan soon after Gerd arrived because by that time I had been in Syria for almost eleven weeks (longer than the Englishwoman on the plane had thought possible), and extending my visa had become a weekly annoyance. Ahmed advised me to leave the country and come back before the immigration authorities denied my all-too-frequent requests to stay just a little bit longer.

We spent a week in the Hashemite Kingdom of Jordan, which Gerd liked better than Syria because it was less dirty, less noisy, and less chaotic. On the twenty-third floor of the Jordan Tower Centre in Amman, we feasted on chicken cordon bleu as we looked out at the capital city built on seven major *jebels* and half a dozen smaller hills. We brought in the Islamic New Year (the *Hegira* lunar calendar is eleven days shorter than the western calendar) quietly at the end of May in Aqaba on the Red Sea. After failing to find a public beach that wasn't swarming with boys splashing and shouting, we stopped into the air-conditioned café of a four-star hotel for a lemonade, and the waiter mistook us for paying guests and ushered us on to their private beach. The drinks cost a fortune and a palm-leaf umbrella leaked sunlight which gave me a burn that later turned my back into layers of tattered lace.

Jordan was more expensive than Syria, which was hard on my budget. The entry for Petra, the rose-coloured capital the Nabateans carved out of rock in pre-Roman times, had gone from one dinar to twenty in the five years since I had last been there. A Jordanian man blamed the price increase on peace with Israel. "The Israelis come here to see Petra," he said, "and they buy nothing. Food, water, benzine—they buy everything in Israel and bring it with them. They leave no money here." Microbus tours allowed crass American college kids to make sorties into Jordan from Israel to see the sights, without learning anything about the culture. After two days of traipsing around Petra, we moved on to Lawrence of Arabia's former haunt, and slept under rough, gritty blankets in an over-priced Bedouin tent tourist-trap, Wadi Rum's only accommodation. Even there, sometimes *marhaba* met with a drawled *shalom*.

We returned to Syria, a land Coca-Cola and Pepsi had not yet invaded, which gave me fifteen days before I had to renew my visa again. We rented a beat-up Beetle which stank of oil and had an irrepressible vent blowing hot air on the driver's right foot. We drove with the windows open, but still the road through the desert was the *highway to hell* for the driver. The summer heat had come early and we joked that the oasis at Palmyra was *green hell.*

In Deir az-Zur we got our first look at *al-Furat,* the Euphrates. The "great river" of the Bible was a muddy straggle of garbage-strewn, putrid, slimy, stagnant water in a concrete trough degraded by faded advertisements with flaking paint. In a café by the river the waiter used a garden hose to soften hard-packed earth, treating us to the frog-like smell of fresh mud, so he could wedge the wobbly table into the ground. The owner's English was limited to "Thank you" and "My God!" and once in a while he shouted the latter in our direction. Above the Euphrates were clouds of mosquitoes demonstrating molecular motion.

Upstream from Deir az-Zur was the real Euphrates, a majestic teal ribbon mentioned in Genesis as one of four rivers flowing out of Eden. Mud huts and bunkers of hay flanked the river. Women bent over in irrigated fields looked like clothes-pins.

Defending a ford in the river is Halabiyah, a third-century fortress founded by Queen Zenobia of Palmyra. Tattered walls, as wide as the road that leads to the castle, start at the river and a series of broken towers converge at the top of a hill. Gerd drove upstream to inspect a Bailey bridge while I climbed to the top of every tower. At the highest point, a shrieking gale raged at the intruder; at the foot of the courtyard, frogs were slimy projectiles plopping into the mud. The Euphrates ripples past the fortress—fluid lives on while stones crumble.

In the rundown centre of Raqqa, on the north bank of the Euphrates, a blunt-faced, dull-eyed teenager whipped a sway-backed, rack-of-ribs lame horse. The brute and the nag—I wanted to shoot them both, put them out of their misery, leave their carcasses to rot in the street, torch the wagon, maybe bury the horse.

We found the two-star Tourism Hotel, which was listed in an Arabic book published by the Ministry of Tourism. The lobby was redolent of cigarette smoke, sweat, and hairspray. The manager met us with a shocked "What you want?" His right hand made a twisting motion as if he were turning an oversized doorknob. Behind him a heavily made-up woman in lime-green Spandex led a man in boxer shorts down a poorly lit hall-way. The man had a slightly bow-legged strut and the woman's hips clanged from one side of the hall to the other. Above us a hard-faced woman in a skimpy top and tight jeans leaned over the banister to look at the foreigners as she put on her belt. A beefy man in a muscle shirt made a brief appearance for a rasping "Welcome in Syria." We didn't bother to look at the rooms even though by western standards the women looked depressingly normal.

We drove on to *Halab*, the Arabic name for Aleppo, which means 'milk' because the city was built where Abraham milked his ewes. We got lost in the *souq* labyrinth of cubbyhole shops: stacks of soap, bolts of cotton, burlap sacks of pistachio nuts and sunflower seeds, the spicy odour of cinnamon, nutmeg, and clove mounds, and the bright yellow glare of saffron. A merchant offered us tea: "Aleppo bestiality—I mean, hospitality. No charge." He recommended a restaurant, saying it served everything we could possibly want, and roast pork (something I don't even like) popped into my head. Later, I fell asleep on the carpet in the Grand Mosque, which has a mausoleum for the head of Zacharias, John the Baptist's father (I didn't know it ran in the family).

In Kassab on the Syrian-Turkish border, we followed signs to an Armenian restaurant at the end of a rough track wedged into a hillside. Gerd and I were the only customers and the owner filled the table with food, saying what we didn't eat, we wouldn't pay for. *Shish tawouck* (chicken), *kibba* (cracked wheat and ground lamb stuffed with minced mutton and pine nuts), *fattoush* (spicy salad greens with pita chips), mutton stuffed pita rolls, French fries, grape leaves stuffed with seasoned rice, crushed chickpeas, mashed eggplant, tomatoes, cucumbers, carrots, olives, onions, cheese puffs—we ate everything.

In Ras al-Bassit we rested, reluctant to move on. The Mediterranean coast was beautiful and quiet; our hotel room came very close to fulfilling both Gerd's quality requirements and my budget constraints. (The budget of a working man on a four-week holiday is incompatible with that of an unemployed woman hoping for an infinite vacation.) We extended our stay one day at a time as destinations fell off the bottom of our shared itinerary, leaving ourselves just enough time for a couple of castles; a couple of convents; and the Isle of Arwad, a rocky reef and the only island in all of Syria.

Saladin's castle—he conquered it after a two-day siege in 1188—is in the mountains that run along the Syrian coast, battleground of Muslims and Crusaders. We drove the Beetle into the bottom of the moat, past a solid rock needle dividing the road. How many calloused hands had chipped, carved, chiselled, hacked a moat out of solid rock, leaving a needle ninety feet high to support a drawbridge? Thorns and hollyhocks and a few stray tourists are heirs to a castle where four thousand soldiers were once stationed. In tall grass, I came across three unmarked holes, each one large enough to swallow a tourist, and dropped stones into the cistern below. Outside the walls, beyond the moat, birds hid in the trees and assaulted the castle with chirpy songs.

Further south Saladin had looked at the mighty Krak des Chevaliers, the Knights' Castle, commanding a strategic pass in the coastal mountains, and withdrew without even attempting a siege. The mighty mediæval fortress was never taken by force. On the 8th of April in 1271, after a month-long siege, three hundred knights of St. John followed the orders of a cleverly forged note, ostensibly from their commander, and surrendered the castle to Muslim forces. Normally, two thousand knights defended the castle. Two thousand knights and a thousand horses, yet neither the latrines nor the stables harbour olfactory relics.

After an hour Gerd retreated to the hotel, which had a beautiful kidney-shaped pool. From the Tower of the Daughter of the King, I took a picture of the Beetle disappearing into terrace-pleated hills. I didn't trust my guidebooks—the circular Master's Keep didn't even make the map in one of them!—so I explored every inch of the castle. My flashlight lit up dens polluted with pop cans and water bottles. Tourists had poisoned the water supply by tossing garbage in the well, and in every dark corner flies swarmed over wads of tissue and piles of putrid shit. Parts of the castle had been desecrated. But not all. I could imagine knights on horseback coming up the triumphant entry ramp; a wild-game feast served under the vaulted arches of the Great Hall; crusaders bowed in prayer in the Chapel, praying for victory, praying for home. I sat in the window of the Master's Keep and tried to capture the Krak des Chevaliers in my journal. After a four-hour siege, I surrendered.

A whirlwind tour. Geographic confusion, roads and villages that didn't exist on any of our maps, creative transliterations, posters plastered over English road signs. Graveyards, convents, monuments, mosques. Missiles guarding the coast. Smug little fishing boats in glossy coats of blues and whites and cadmium yellows. Date palms, fig trees, snapdragons, sunflowers. And through it all there were kisses and quarrels, tight hugs and caresses. Sometimes we argued, picking at details, while studiously avoiding: why won't you rearrange your life to be with me, here, now, always? Yet knowing that neither of us really wanted that anyway. Distance provides balance. One night Gerd dreamt we were travelling and many snakes got loose. We rounded up the little snakes and put them in clay pots, but a large snake, possibly poisonous, eluded us. Gerd rarely remembers dreams. We both cried at the airport when he left to go back to Canada. Offa and Ahmed were surprised that I didn't go with him.

✦ *summer*

A friend living in the Caribbean told me that Haiti has only two temperatures: hot and damn hot. By her reckoning, I would say that Canada has three—hot, cold, and damn cold—and Syria has three as well: cold, hot, and damn hot. By the time Gerd left, Syria was damn hot.

In the spring Huda had told me Damascus was very pleasant in the summer. This rather surprised me since I knew that wealthy Damascenes, including Huda's family, had summer homes in Bludan or Zabadani in the mountains near the Lebanese border because it's cooler there in the summer. I asked her what she meant by "pleasant."

"Palmyra, the whole desert, is *very* hot, but here in Damascus, it's pleasant. Even if it's forty-three degrees, you can still sleep at night." She was serious.

"Forty-three degrees! I will die." The only explanation I could see for thinking that forty-three degrees Celsius was anything other than damn hot was that Huda had once taught school in Tunisia. I told her I had experienced forty-three below zero, never above.

"Forty-three below zero! I will die," she gasped. She was serious about that, too.

In the chill of winter and the pale warmth of early spring, I had waited for the sun to peer out from behind the mosque by my house. Tying back the gingham curtain in the kitchen, I had welcomed the sun into my home. In the summer, the sun came striding out from behind the mosque in mid-morning and I felt as if a friend had betrayed me. I yanked the curtain shut, thinking, I don't want that wench in my house.

Unlike Huda, I had trouble sleeping at night when it was hot. The fridge, which was in the bedroom because the kitchen was small, droned like a low-flying airplane on a transatlantic flight. The heat, the fridge, and a rasping three-speed electric fan manufacturing a breeze made sleep elusive.

I made a list of reasons to like the heat: laundry dries fast; butter isn't too hard even if you forget to take it out of the fridge early; I like ice cream; afternoon naps are condoned. I lay on the bed and tried to remember skating on a frozen pond, or the throbbing pain of toes thawing. I began to despise the sun. One afternoon I wrote: *Sweat is the snaking tongue of the devil licking my ribs. The sun weighs me down, presses me into the sidewalk. Razes my body, scalds my brain. It claws at my skin till my bones shrivel and sap runs out of a charred soul.*

In the summer, Syria is damn hot, and Huda went to Paris to stay with friends. I'm sure she had no trouble sleeping.

⬛ *visas*

Tourist visas expire. With Ahmed's help, I had extended mine several times, discreetly pressing larger and larger thank-you-for-smoothing-the-way bills into the palm of "my" official at the Immigration Office in Damascus. He shepherded my applications through four floors of bureaucratic chaos. All I had to do was buy stamps, fill out a French-Arabic form in quadruplicate (without the benefit of a carbon), and get the chief to sign a stamped copy.

The chief was a bulky man with gold stars on his broad shoulders and five telephones, including two red ones, on his massive desk. I had spent three months in Syria when I ventured into his office for the last time, after timidly knocking on the door—I felt like a schoolgirl. The chief scowled at my application to stay one more month for an eternity before signing it. Then he threw it and my passport to the far side of his massive desk with a disgusted grunt. I gathered my papers and retreated. The chief never even looked at me.

Both Ahmed and my official thought it unlikely that I

could get another extension. I had already done the leave-the-country-and-come-back trick (my lover and I had spent a week in Jordan and my multiple entry visa had since expired), and for that last extension Ahmed had requested that I put down the name of a hotel as my address. I understood that I had worn out my welcome. I didn't want to get anyone into trouble. I had a few weeks left to travel.

◼ Quneitra

Zabadani, Zabadani! Halab! Quneitra! Drivers shouted destinations. A birdlike boy tried to sell me a newspaper. I told him I couldn't read it, it was too difficult for me. He stood in the door of the Quneitra *meecro* and read the headings on the passenger list out loud: name, father's name, mother's name, year of birth, destination, ID. His whole body shook as he laughed at names like Robert and Mary-Jo written in my laborious Arabic script.

When all fourteen seats were full, a policeman took the passenger list and the white *meecro* van honked its way out of Damascus and headed south. A few kilometres north of Quneitra in the Golan Heights, I transferred to a garish Scania bus that smelled like dirt and motor oil and engine grease. Garlands of silk roses and plastic bananas swayed from the ceiling.

At the third police checkpoint on the way to Quneitra, I gave the special permit issued by the U.N. Office in Damascus to a middle-aged swarthy man, who disappeared with it. A few minutes later a young man with an auburn pompadour got on the bus. He was well dressed: wine-coloured trousers, matching patterned shirt, expensive leather shoes. He sat down beside me and I realized he was holding my permit.

The bus drove through the checkpoint. Over the roar of the motor, the young man shouted, "Do you speak Arabic?"

"A little," I said.

"Good." He looked relieved. "I will visit Quneitra with you."

"No, I will visit the city alone." I reached for the permit and he moved it away.

Chuckling, he repeated that he would visit Quneitra with me.

"I want to visit Quneitra alone," I said firmly. "I want my permit."

He jerked back his head, raised his eyebrows, and lowered his eyelids in refusal. The bus stopped and he got up to leave, with my permit in hand. He waved for me to follow, and I did. We were the only ones to get off and the bus rumbled away, leaving us with a trail of diesel smoke in a deserted traffic circle. I looked around: concrete roofs lay like hardcover books opened face-down on rubble; a petrified accordion stairway ran haphazardly up to the sky. Every house had been flattened. There was no one in sight. I was alone with a cocky young man I had no reason to trust. Hollywood movies convince Syrian men that western women are enthusiastically promiscuous. Of course, by the standards set for Muslim women in the Middle East, we are!

The young man started down a dirt road lined with bushes and beckoned for me to follow. I stood my ground in the traffic circle, nervously tapping a hiking boot on the pavement. "I'm not going with you," I snapped. I didn't want a male escort dogging me through the ruins, asking inane questions while trying to jockey himself into position to accidentally brush his arm against my breasts. In halting Arabic I ordered him to hand over the permit and leave me alone. He tried to cajole me into accompanying him. Folding my arms over my chest, I threw back my head, lowered my eyelids, and clicked my tongue in refusal. He was shaken, but he stayed with me. He wouldn't leave me alone.

"Who are you?" I demanded. None of this would be happening if Gerd were here, I thought, and he's only been gone a couple of days. Inwardly I felt like a coward for wanting to hide in his shadow; outwardly I sounded like a drill sergeant.

"Khaled," he said.

I repeated his name contemptuously. The best defence is an offence. "Who are you?" I barked.

"Khaled."

I glared at him.

Khaled looked down at his black leather shoes. After some hesitation, he looked up and quietly added, "Police."

With his puffy hair and elegant clothes, he looked more like a disco clown. Surprise flitted across my face and he warmed up to his explanation a little too quickly. "Yes, police. I am police."

I challenged him to show me ID.

"I am police." He pleaded with me. I showed no mercy. "Photo ID." I held out my hand imperiously.

Reluctantly he pulled his wallet out of his back pocket. After looking around to be sure there was no one in sight, he flipped it open and produced a laminated ID card with a picture. I brazenly checked the photograph against his face: grey eyes, thin nose dusted with freckles, auburn hair, puffed up more in real life than in the picture. It was him.

"Where does it say police?" My scanning abilities in Arabic were next to nil; I didn't want to be taken in on a bluff.

Khaled pointed to a word and said, "Mukhabarat." A trump card. My body stiffened. Sliding my index finger across the plastic from right to left, I deciphered the cursive script. He wasn't just "police," he was mukhabarat—secret police! Defiance melted into deference. "Mukhabarat," I said slowly, nodding deeply.

"Yes. *Mukhabarat.*" He nodded deeply and smiled as he tucked his wallet and my permit into the back pocket of his maroon trousers. He led the way down the dirt road lined with bushes, and I followed.

We came to the Golan Hospital, scarred by shelling. Hideous pocks on blackened basalt. An English sign read: "Destructed by Zionists and changed it to firing target." Inside, shelling had perforated plaster walls which had once reached to the ceiling. Khaled encouraged me to take pictures of the ruined building.

Israel captured the Golan Heights in the Arab-Israeli war of 1967. Before turning the city of Quneitra over to U.N. forces in 1974, Israeli soldiers evacuated the people who lived there, dismantled whatever they could—doors, windows, light fixtures, and so on—and sold the booty to Israeli contractors. Bulldozers and target practise destroyed what was left. Israel claimed that Quneitra had been destroyed earlier, during the fighting. Photographs showed the city intact during the Israeli occupation. The General Assembly of the United Nations condemned Israel for the deliberate destruction of Quneitra.

As Khaled and I wandered around the ruined city, he slipped questions into seemingly innocuous conversations. How long had I been in Syria? Where was I staying? Where did I study Arabic? What was my work? And thrown in after "Do you drink beer?" and "Do you drink whiskey?" was an unnaturally casual, "Have you been to Israel?" The wrong answer could get a foreigner expelled from Syria. "No," I said and held myself back from an equally casual, "Have you?" (Technically it wasn't a lie because the Arab world maintains that Jerusalem and the West Bank are not part of Israel.)

I asked Khaled a few questions, too. Did he live in the nearby village of Khan Arnabah? He scoffed. The idea was too ludicrous. Of course not! He lived in Damascus. How old was he? Twenty-five. Was he married? No. Had he travelled outside Syria? No, not yet. He wanted to, though.

The questions I wanted to ask, I left unspoken. What's it like to be *mukhabarat*? Is this a normal day for you? Do you belong to the Alawite Muslim faith like President Assad? (A powerful religious minority rules a significant Sunni Muslim majority.) What kind of training do you have? Do your friends know what you do for a living? When you're *mukhabarat* can you actually *have* friends? Does your *mother* know?

I had nothing to hide and presumably nothing to fear. Khaled seemed friendly. He was young, and male: he might have been flattered by my curiosity. Why didn't I ask those questions? Because he was *mukhabarat*. He had the power to raise a red flag. I had a Canadian passport, of course—I was safe. But Khaled had the power to make the lives of my Syrian friends miserable. I knew better than to rock the boat. You just don't mess with the *mukhabarat*.

I couldn't forget where the money to pay for Khaled's expensive leather shoes had come from. Neither could he. The sight of police officers in the centre of the ruined city prompted him to say, "They are police. *We* are *mukhabarat*." The pecking order of authority.

Khaled showed me a ruptured bank and the gutted ghost of a church. Using my camera, he took a picture of me in front of the bank. It was okay to take pictures of the ruins and even of Israel across the border. It was not okay to take pictures of the army or anything military and he refused to let me photograph him.

At a military cemetery, the Arab Martyrs Graveyard, an elderly Dutch couple was inspecting the graves. A chauffeur waited by their rental car, an air-conditioned Mercedes Benz. Another man stood in the shade of a monument, watching them. "*Mukhabarat?*" I whispered. Khaled nodded curtly and went to join him. I overheard the man ask Khaled whether I spoke Arabic. He said no. My Arabic was feeble—I was under no illusions about that—but Khaled and I hadn't spoken a word in any other language.

After stops at a museum, two cemeteries, and a Friendship Garden full of scrawny saplings planted by people from around the world, Khaled was tired. He was used to travelling by car and we were on foot. He complained about the heat. I showed him a thermometer attached to the zipper on my day pack. A cold front had moved in the day before—it was only thirty degrees. I offered him my hat, but he declined. It would have flattened his puffy hairdo. "Finished?" he said hopefully.

I wanted to see the mosque.

"There. You see it." Protruding above the rubble in the centre of the city was a forlorn minaret, damaged by shelling. "Finished?"

"I want to *visit* the mosque."

The walls were still standing; the roof was a grid of steel rafters. There were no carpets—just bare concrete, rubble and dust. "Finished?" Khaled said again.

"No." The doorway to the minaret was open. A spiral staircase curled out of sight. Khaled hesitated before insisting that he go first. The stairway was dark. Our fingers crept along the curving concrete wall as our shoes pushed aside rubble and sank into powder which sifted into our nostrils. Khaled paused again and again, muttering to himself, then glancing over his shoulder at me and saying things I couldn't understand. He was nervous, almost annoyed, poised on the edge of fear. It was clearly the first time he had braved the minaret. I responded with "*tfaddal*"—as you like, if you please—and stayed close behind him so he couldn't use me as an excuse to turn back.

At the top of the stairs we stepped out into sunlight. We lingered on the platform where the *muezzin* would have stood (before cassette recordings nudged him out of the way), calling the believers to prayer five times a day. Khaled lit a cigarette. The emotions he had struggled with in the stairwell were hidden under a veneer of quiet confidence. With one foot resting on a solid chunk of the balustrade—shells had blasted some sections into oblivion—he looked like a cigarette advertisement. His

right arm rested on his knee. His fancy black shoes were pow-
dered white. He surveyed the remnants of the city and, without
turning towards me, asked, "Beautiful?"

Syrians often see beauty in places western eyes have to
battle with filth or rubble to uncover the beauty a Syrian natu-
rally sees. Quneitra lay below us in a desolate panorama of
collapsed roofs, broken walls, demolished homes. Oleander
bushes had taken root in the rubble. Across the border in Israel,
the top of the closest mountain was covered in radio towers and
satellite dish receivers.

"No," I said, laughing. "Quneitra is not beautiful. Maybe
it was, but now it is not." I gave it the benefit of the doubt.
Looking at the concrete debris, I suspected it had never been
beautiful, at least not in modern times.

Khaled laughed, too. He stubbed his cigarette out on the
balustrade and flicked the butt through a hole in the railing.
Then, turning to me, he said, "Finished?"

The day had gone just as Khaled had said: he visited
Quneitra with me and he kept my permit. We parted at a police
checkpoint; he got off the bus and I stayed on. I had lunch in
Khan Arnabah, sharing a table with two women whose brown
hands ripped apart a greasy chicken on a newspaper platter. The
women motioned for me to join their feast but I turned them
down. As I ate my felafel sandwich, I wondered whether Khaled
had a report to write. If he did, I'll bet our stand-off in the
traffic circle didn't get a mention.

▧ a night in Dara'a

Dara'a is a nondescript town in southern Syria that long ago warranted a mention in the Old Testament as Edrei, the royal city of Og, conquered by Moses and the Israelites. Modern Dara'a wangles its way into guidebooks by being the last town in Syria before the border crossing into Jordan. As an aside, my guidebook said Dara'a could be used as a base for a day trip to the town of Bosra, which boasts a Roman theatre and no budget hotels. That's why I went to Dara'a.

I got a ticket for an air-conditioned Karnak bus that would leave Damascus at a scheduled time instead of whenever the bus was full. The day before I was supposed to leave for Dara'a, I visited Quneitra. That night, I couldn't get to sleep. Too hot, I thought. Then I felt sick. From midnight till dawn, my stomach and bowels made it absolutely clear that they didn't want any part of the Khan Arnabah felafel sandwich or anything else I had eaten that day. Refusing to believe my favourites could be guilty, I absolved a chocolate shake and a banana split from a two-star café in Damascus of any wrong doing in the matter. I laid the blame squarely on my bargain lunch of ground chickpeas, deep-fried and then hand-crushed and tucked into a pita bread pocket with overripe tomatoes. The sweaty chef had wrapped the felafel lovingly in newsprint. By the time I reached the dry heaves stage, well before the early morning call to the mosque, I was cursing the no-star food stand in Khan Arnabah.

The next day I lay on the bed feeling weak and sorry for myself in the moments I was awake. The urgent nature of the illness had caused me to leave the light on in the bathroom to serve as a beacon. There was no time to fumble around in the dark, looking for a light switch. I woke up once, saw the light on, thought Gerd must have forgotten to turn it off, and wondered where he was. When I remembered he was gone, a flood of loneliness made me feel even more wretched. To cheer myself up, I tried to look at the bright side of food poisoning: firstly, not eating for a day was good for my budget (since I would have to buy another bus ticket); secondly, after each bout in the bathroom I had felt chilled, which was a definite bonus in the summer in Syria; thirdly, I had been ill in the clean and secure surroundings of my own little house in Damascus. While I sipped flattened ginger ale and counted my blessings, I missed the bus to Dara'a.

A couple of days later I felt better and my landlady Offa had me over for lunch. She lectured me yet again on the hazards of eating just anywhere, while I fattened myself up on *kibba*— cracked wheat dumplings stuffed with onions and minced mutton—and rice clotted in goats' milk. After lunch Ahmed drove me to the Karnak station and I caught the bus to Dara'a.

I arrived in mid-afternoon, when it was, to put it mildly, *really* hot. A young woman and I took refuge in a scrap of shade to arrange our bags. She was well dressed according to the standards of her religion, poorly dressed for the heat. A dark robe reached to her feet, which were clad in dark stockings and black dress shoes. Black gloves covered her hands, and a black scarf concealed her hair and forehead. Only her eyes showed, because a black cloth pinned to her scarf defended the rest of her face from the indignity of being ravished by the eyes of unknown men and infidels. The skin around her eyes was bathed in perspiration.

I was wearing a Tilley hat, a high-necked, long-sleeved white blouse, a khaki Tilley skirt to mid-calf, and clunky hiking boots with thick socks rolled over to cover the laces, to keep them from dragging in the dirt. The same outfit prompted a Dutch traveller, who was wearing a skirt made out of a flour sack, to take my picture in the ruins of a desert palace because I looked like a "turn-of-the-century lady archaeologist."

The Muslim woman watched as I hoisted my backpack onto my knee, swung it onto my back and clicked the waist and chest buckles into place. I could only see her eyes, yet it seemed to me that those eyes promised more beauty than a face stripped bare to the wind could ever fulfill.

My guidebook mentioned only one hotel in Dara'a. It was supposed to be north of the post office. Outside the bus station, an Arab man wearing a jaunty hat gave me directions to the post office. The man was on a one-speed bicycle and he weaved alongside me for a bit. We passed a park where the uplifted beaks of four swans in a fountain pointed to the corners of the earth.

"Beautiful," I said.

The man sneered. "It's for Bassel Assad. Many people are angry. The park cost one hundred million Syrian pounds, and so many people are hungry."

I was shocked, but not at the price. Criticism of the government was more incredible than two million U.S. dollars. Bassel Assad, the President's late son, seemed ready for sainthood. He was referred to as *shaheed* (martyr) so often it was easy to forget he died in a high-speed car accident in thick fog near the Damascus airport, not in a battle against Zionists. Pictures of Bassel were everywhere, including the living room of my house in Damascus. His air-conditioned mausoleum in the President's home town of al-Qardaha had become a shrine. To say anything negative about Bassel Assad was equivalent to blasphemy. The cyclist's loose lips made me nervous and I let the subject drop.

At the end of a wide avenue that led to the post office, the man took his leave from me. "Welcome," he said, "but I cannot say 'Welcome in my country.' I am Palestinian. When I return to the West Bank and you visit there, then I will say 'Welcome in my country.'" He tipped his jaunty hat and cycled away.

I looked for a hotel north of the post office and found nothing. I asked for help and a soldier waved me back to a big hotel just south of the post office, although he looked disconcerted at my choice of hotel and suggested another one. But I stuck by my guidebook because Syrians usually recommend expensive hotels to foreigners. The guidebook said the budget hotel was a "big place," "north of the post office" with "no name in English." Except for the direction, this one fit the bill so I assumed the writer had a faulty compass. The Arabic sign said Riyadhi Tourist.

Inside, it seemed that a lone female backpacker asking for a room was not an everyday occurrence. The manager responded to my request with a surprised "Here?" Once he realized that I was serious, he and the other staff gathered for the occasion were eager, if not exactly the "friendly" my guidebook promised. I asked for a room at the back, away from the street. At three o'clock in the afternoon on a summer day, every street in Syria is quiet. I had made the mistake elsewhere of assuming that a quiet street stayed that way when the sun went down.

The manager sent a cigarette-smoking boy with a withered left arm crooked at his side to show me a room. Upstairs, we passed an open doorway. A woman with long black hair hanging loose over her shoulders sat on a bed, singing softly to herself. She was dressed in jeans and a tank top. Both her hair and her arms were bare. Cigarette smoke veiled her face. The sun must have addled my brains for I took it to be a good sign that an Arab woman was staying in the hotel, and I didn't even question her attire.

The boy showed me room number thirteen. There were two single beds with brown blankets, and a weary bedside table splattered with paint. The ceiling was fourteen feet high; sticky cobwebs attached it to clay-coloured high-gloss walls and there were spiders plotting in the corners. A fluorescent light tube was suspended on a heavy chain thick with dust, and curtainless windows faced west for the full warmth of the evening sun. The air in the room was stale—headache material. There was no fan and a cockroach was cutting across a dirty white tile on the chequerboard floor, moving towards the bed. I snapped its body under my hiking boot and squashed it into the floor.

"*Malesh*," the boy said. Never mind.

He was right. There were more important things.

"Do the windows open?"

"Of course!" He threw open the windows and flicked ashes into the courtyard.

The room next door was pretty much the same, except it didn't have a lock, so I traded my passport for the key to room number thirteen. When I went to leave the room, however, I found that the key didn't do me a lot of good. I couldn't lock the door behind me. I pulled at the door; I turned and twisted the key until my fingers ached. All for naught. I couldn't lock the door. The woman down the hall tried. The manager tried. Another man tried. Finally the boy with the bad arm, dangling a cigarette in his mouth and extending his baby finger to flaunt a ridiculously long fingernail, which presumably showed he was unaccustomed to manual labour, took the key. With some magic manoeuvre and what looked like an effortless turn of the key, he succeeded where the rest of us had failed. The door was finally locked.

The lad was immensely proud of himself and I fawned

over him accordingly until he brushed me aside like a boy king refusing an audience. He deigned to give me my key, then he took a drag off his cigarette, puffed his little chest out, and strutted regally down the hall.

I left the hotel and wandered around in the streets of Dara'a. I bought a cola in a grubby restaurant. When a man at the next table got a felafel, the smell made me gag. I retreated to the curb. Next door was a *shawarma* stand, where hunks of lamb twirled on a vertical spit. It was a sauna for flies.

I withdrew to the Bassel Assad park the Palestinian man had sneered at. A breeze and a fountain conspired to offer misty caresses. Distorted Arabic music came from a nearby playground and snack bar. Schoolgirls joined me and we looked at every picture in my guidebook. A snub-nosed girl solemnly declared every mosque, even the most austere, to be that of Sayyida Zeinab. When we came to the one that was, she took the book out of my hands and spent several minutes admiring the chandeliers and Las Vegas-style glitter of Sayyida Zeinab's Mausoleum on the outskirts of Damascus.

A girl with her hair in a tight ponytail recognized the theatre at Bosra. I asked her whether she had visited it. She said *no* and threw me a look as if to say: what a ridiculous question! You would have thought I had asked whether she had been to the moon. She told me she had seen the theatre in books at school. I decided not to tell her I would see the real thing tomorrow.

After the schoolgirls left, a charming woman named Moona joined me, and by the time she left with her aunt and her sister and her sister's fiancé, it was well after dark.

I went back to the Riyadhi Tourist Hotel and couldn't get into my room. The boy king had to be called out to unlock the door. The manager came by a few minutes later, anxious that I pay. He had my passport as a hostage; I didn't see how I could skip without paying, but I gave him money for one night and he returned my passport.

My room was still hot, but with the windows open, the air was reasonably fresh—unlike what I had smelled at the end of the hall. The toilet was the kind you could find blindfolded and I had to use it. The pit was a hole in the floor—a stinking ceramic bowl shaped like an oversized bicycle seat. Modern pit toilets flush—this one didn't. A tap and a plastic water bottle with the top cut off served as the cleaning mechanism for both the toilet and the user of the toilet. Toilet paper was too much to expect. I was accustomed, however, to having a hose or at least a proper jug as the water source. No such luxury in that hotel.

Back in my room, I tried to lock the door for the night. I lost the battle and consoled myself with the thought that I wouldn't have to fight to get out in the morning. The beat-up bedside table with my backpack on top of it served as a mini barricade, and for the first time, I set up a battery-operated door alarm my mother had given me to ease her worries. If anyone jiggled the door or tried to open it, a high-pitched, excruciatingly loud alarm would sound.

Satisfied with my fortifications to the door, I turned my attention to the beds. There were two to choose from. Each had one itchy brown blanket and one grey sheet, soiled with stains and dirt from who knew how many unwashed tours of duty. I chose what looked to be the better bed and stripped it down to the mattress. I got my sleeping sack (a sheet sewn up as a sleeping bag with a pouch for a pillow) out of my backpack and spread it over the bed. The bed was usable. The mattress was almost comfortable. I decided to sleep with the light on because I didn't even want to think about what kinds of bugs would come out under cover of darkness.

I was in bed, starting to drift off to sleep before eleven. After eleven, the band started. Live music, amply amplified, reverberated from the ground floor at the back of the hotel. Drums, strings, and a flute. Sleep was impossible. So much for my care in choosing a back room to avoid street noise. I considered getting dressed and going downstairs, but I didn't want to leave my backpack in an unlocked room and having to get help to lock my door was a deterrent. Besides, the music was plenty loud in my room. I could feel the bass notes in my chest.

A singer, most likely the bare-armed woman from down the hall, joined the band. Her voice, arcing over the torrent of music, was strained from overuse or too much tobacco. While she wailed, drums rattled and boomed, strings soared and swooped and squealed like swallows, and a flute hovered and fluttered like pigeon murmurs. Between songs, the gentle hum of men's voices lulled me to sleep. But the singer always cut through, urging the band onwards: "*Yellah!*" Let's go. And they were off into another frenzy of Arabic birdsong. I understood why the manager had been so anxious for me to pay early.

The band played until after three in the morning, and then the singer and musicians came upstairs to unwind. I could hear them laughing and telling stories down the hall. A man called out "*al-ajnabiya hone*"—the foreign woman is here—no doubt pointing at the door to room number thirteen.

At three twenty-five the early morning call to the mosque filled the air. *Allah akbar!* God is great. Sometime around four o'clock silence wrapped its cloak around me and I fell asleep.

In less than an hour a scream sliced through my sleep. I woke up at the door with the alarm screaming in my hand. I was still in my sleeping sack with a pillow tucked under one arm. With shaky fingers I disabled the alarm. The door was still shut. I heard a man's voice, then the hotel fell silent. All I could hear was my own heart hammering against my chest. I breathed a sigh of relief that my barricade hadn't been put to the test, yet I couldn't go back to sleep.

With less than an hour of sleep, I was in no shape to go sightseeing in Bosra. Even if I could find another hotel and sleep for a few hours, the day was a write-off, for I would have slept through the coolest part of the day and been sightseeing in the hottest. I decided to go back to Damascus, where I had a clean and quiet place to stay. A rooster crowed; it was nearly morning. The cool air was delicious. As I dressed and packed, dawn disrobed the darkness.

I dismantled the barricade and with the door alarm in my hand, I left my unlucky room. I crept along the hall and down the stairs, gaining confidence when I saw the lobby was empty. Fear is a dreadful feeling which so often turns to spite, anger, and revenge: when I crossed the threshold and felt safe, I deliberately set off my alarm, hoping to shatter the sleep of the music-makers. I lingered by the doorway for a moment, letting the siren rip the silence to shreds.

I caught a bus back to Damascus, where I put my alarm away and slept in silent safety. I told Offa and Ahmed about the loud music, but I didn't say anything about the door not having a lock or the need for an alarm. Later I visited the Roman theatre at Bosra as a day trip from Damascus. I never went back to Dara'a, but I remember it well. Moona, the charming woman who joined me in the park, made a night in Dara'a worthwhile.

▨ I remember Moona

In the small city of Dara'a in the south of Syria, there is a park. In the park there is a fountain, and in the fountain there are swans as tall as the palm trees. In that park I met Moona.

An opal moon hung in a velvet sky, a rainbow of lights lit the swans, and Moona joined me on a park bench, filling me with the scent of her rose-water perfume. She was wearing a long-sleeved cream chiffon tunic, a pleated skirt, white stockings, and black suede shoes with gold buckles. A white scarf covered her hair. In a voice as rich as chocolate, she asked whether I spoke Arabic. I said I could speak it a little, and her eyes, set in a skin of magnolias, sparkled like mica.

Moona was twenty. She had finished school and was living at home without looking for work. When I asked whether she was married, she laughed and replied, "*Abadan*. Never. I'm free."

She was in the park with Rana, her twenty-three-year-old aunt. The women were chaperoning Moona's sister, who was nearby with her fiancé. Moona pointed them out when they passed us. In good fun, she mimicked her swashbuckling brother-in-law-to-be. He and Moona's sister walked side by side, circling the swans. They didn't touch; there was plenty of room to throw a cat between them.

Moona told me they had met at a party where her sister had served him something to drink and smiled at him. He contacted her parents and asked for her hand. He was a good Muslim and a good provider, and she had no objections, so her parents said yes. The couple had known each other for three weeks, and in another three weeks they would be married.

Moona's aunt Rana was in love with a Palestinian man she had met at an English institute in Jordan. They had known each other for five years and wanted to marry. They planned to have only two children and he said it wouldn't matter if both were girls. But he wasn't "prosperous" yet and her parents had rejected him. Rana's eyes filled with tears. He would work hard and try again. I blanched at the thought of my parents accepting or rejecting someone on my behalf.

Rana had heard that in America a man and a woman sometimes lived in the same house before they were married. I confirmed that it was true. I didn't tell her I had done it myself and not married the man. She adjusted her headscarf and fiddled with the gold buttons on the front of her dark green robe. "Does it happen in your country, too?" she asked.

"Yes, it's very common. Does it happen here?" I knew the answer. I just wanted to see her reaction to the question.

Rana clutched her chest and reeled as if she were having a heart attack. "*Abadan!* Never! If a woman goes with a man before she is married, her father will kill her." So-called honour killings. Rana's hand sliced across her throat and her head flopped forward as if she were dead. Moona brought her back to life by tugging at her sleeve for an Arabic translation. I felt bad about toying with Rana like that. She got up to walk for a bit, leaving Moona and me alone.

Moona didn't speak much English, yet she was eager to practise what she knew. She enunciated her schoolgirl phrases as clearly as a well-trained Eliza Doolittle. In reply to "thank you," she sang out "not at all" as a descending arpeggio.

"Excuse me," she said, "is that your bag?" and her kohl-lined eyes shone with excitement.

"Yes, that is my bag. Is that your bag?" I asked, pointing at a palm tree.

"No. That is not my bag." She replied as graciously as an English princess, yet she threw her head back, raised her eyebrows, and closed her eyes momentarily, using her own Arab body language to underline the negative. Then her mascara-webbed lashes flew up, for she was eager to see if I was as delighted with her response as she. I was. She was enchanting. With Moona there would always be laughter. I couldn't help but think what her social life might have been like had she grown up without the sobering influence of her culture and Islam.

After Moona and I had giggled and laughed for a long time, she became serious. As her sister spiralled ever closer to matrimony and water splashed on the glistening bosoms of the swans, Moona drew me close. I inhaled her sweet perfume like a honeybee nestled in rose petals. Her eyes looked into mine and from her lips, in English like silk, came ribbons of Christina Georgina Rossetti, a nineteenth-century poet. "Remember," she said. " 'Remember me when I am gone away,/ Gone far away into the silent land.' "

Her words surprised me, moved me, and I believe she knew what she was saying. Yet even if she didn't, it doesn't really matter. I did and I remember.

Under a girasol moon, I remember Moona.

◙ *fear*

Racing the downward stroke of an axe is an idiotic thing to do. I tried it once—twice, actually. I won the first round and lost the second, along with part of a finger. I was young, just three and a half years old—and fearless. What's my excuse for getting into a car with Srouran (a man enraged by godmothers the last time I had seen him) when he drove up in a big fat Mercedes with a pair of steel handcuffs and the leather strap of a wooden club around the gearshift? I was neither young nor fearless.

Father's Day was coming up and I wanted to get my dad a fancy halter for his horse. Srouran was an avid equestrian, and in an English lesson a couple of months earlier, we had talked about riding gear—I found out from him that the word 'hackamore' comes from Arabic (via Spanish)—and he had offered to show me the *Souq Saruja*, the harness market in the Old City. And Srouran, who had gotten a discount for his lessons, owed me money. When I got back from Dara'a, I called him and he agreed to pay, and he also agreed to take me to the

Souq Saruja to get a halter for my father's horse. Srouran was a big man, bull-like. I pitied his horse.

He picked me up the next morning, and my neighbour, a round old man parked on a three-legged stool in the shade in front of his carpentry shop, scowled at my responding to the horn of a gleaming black Mercedes. My lover had only been gone a few days: I knew what the old man was thinking.

Sometime between opening the car door and sinking into the soft leather of the passenger seat, I saw handcuffs and a wooden club, but I got into the car anyway. The mind hesitates to inform the body about things beyond reason: handcuffs, truncheons; a severed finger lying in the dirt. The body continues with what it was doing. When the message arrives, it's too late.

I shut the door and Srouran put the car into gear. Handcuffs are circles of confinement, entrapment. Driving down Adnan al-Malki Street, which leads *away* from the *souq*, my heart pounded the way it did when I was a little girl, hemmed in by dirt walls, frozen on the rock-slab steps of the root cellar, which in my mind didn't have room for bottled vegetables because it was chock-a-block full of musty cobwebs and spiders. Fear has a way of focussing life, capturing every dimension. From behind smoked glass I looked out at the street: wrought-iron balconies leered like cages; a garbage bin loomed like a rotting prison cell; tortured palm trees, machete fronds hacking up freedom. Last seen by my neighbour, I thought, who now thinks I'm a whore.

Srouran's meaty hands punched the horn as he steered the car through traffic. The silence in the car was oppressive. If only Srouran would talk, maybe everything would be okay. Words were cardboard tokens cutting into my mouth. I spat out wads, splutters of polite conversation. How was business in his father's shoe store? Had he been riding lately? His answers were short, blunt, snuffing out further enquiries.

We whirled around the traffic circle at al-Umawiyeen

Square. The fountain gushed. The screech of the traffic cop's whistle caught like a scream in my throat. I held my breath, afraid of the exit that led into naked hills riddled with root-cellar caves, which in my mind couldn't have room for ancient scrolls because they were chock-a-block full of bodies. Rotting flesh, mouldering bones. Girls who were never found. And thirty-seven-year-old idiots!

Srouran lit a cigarette. His thumb, which was half the size of my wrist, made a flame leap out of his gold lighter. His eyes squinted as he inhaled. He closed the lighter with a deliberate snap. The lid came down like a guillotine. We stopped at a traffic light near a movie theatre with posters proclaiming: EVIL HAS NEVER BEEN MORE EROTIC. I wanted to jump out, run through the traffic screaming. But he hadn't *done* anything. Innocent until proven guilty. Did I have to wait? Smoke hung in the air like entrails.

We drove through the core of the city. At last I was almost sure he was indeed taking me to the *souq*. I gained courage. I pointed at the steel handcuffs wrapped around the gearshift. "What's this?" I tried to sound nonchalant. Men are like horses: never let them know you're afraid.

"Nothing." He spoke quietly—with what seemed like an arrogant disregard for the havoc he had wreaked. Without even looking at me or the manacles, he bludgeoned my question into silence.

In the *Souq Saruja*, planks of dust-speckled sunlight fell through holes in the roof. Merchants clicked prayer beads and chaffered through shivers of Arabic music. A small window in the back of a saddlemaker's shop looked out at the Barada River, which emerged from under the market.

Srouran marched around the *souq* like he owned the place. Fear gave way to relief hobbled with resentment. Perhaps Srouran was a kind, good-hearted, gentle man who just happened to carry handcuffs and a club around in his car. More likely he was *mukhabarat*—a bully with authority.

He tried to pull me past a poor man's shop of woollen halters in favour of one that was rich with the heavy odour of leather. I resisted. The shop I favoured was small: a boy sitting cross-legged covered the floor. His fingers were in the midst of creation—braid, twist, poke, thread—and his art hung on the walls above him in a jumble of tassels and beads. The colours were alive in a blaze of fiery arpeggios clamouring to be seen, not heard. I picked out a chord that would look good on my father's bay gelding, and I used the money Srouran owed me to pay for it.

Outside the *souq*, Srouran expected me to get back in the car with him. I declined. I said I wanted to poke around the Old City for a while and would take a *meecro* home. His eyebrows shot up in surprise, but he didn't make a fuss. We said good-bye and he drove away in the big fat Mercedes with a pair of steel handcuffs and the leather strap of a wooden club around the gearshift.

I only got into that car with Srouran once. I guess I learned something between the ages of three and thirty-seven.

▧ *a deliberate accident*

What follows happened immediately after I said good-bye to Srouran outside the *Souq Saruja*. A coincidence, perhaps.

At the post office in the modern part of Damascus, a customs officer inspected the halter I had bought for my father and an independent wrapper stitched it into a parcel. I paid the wrapper, bought stamps, mailed the parcel, and then returned to the market area. Traffic was scarce. The Old City wasn't built for cars.

Srouran dominated my thoughts: my English student was possibly a shoe salesman and almost certainly *mukhabarat*. Walking along in the shade of the Citadel, I tried to remember everything I had ever told him. Had I mentioned Huda by name? Had I told him what I paid for Arabic lessons? Then, for some reason—fate I suppose—I had an urge to see the Barada River on the north side of the street. I tried to talk myself out of it: by the time the Barada reached that side of Damascus, it was a grey, disgusting, pitiful excuse for a river; it had turned my stomach once to see a vegetable merchant washing his produce in its waters; and, to see the river I had to leave the shade; I had to walk into the sun. Logic wasn't enough.

Stepping into the sun, I crossed the deserted street and climbed onto a low sidewalk by an iron fence above the river. The air smelled like old dishwater. A pair of white panties with black lace drifted past bags of rubbish clogging the stream. Over the sound of the river gargling and choking on garbage, I heard the buzz of a motorcycle. I glanced over my shoulder. A police officer wearing the sand-coloured summer uniform was coming around the corner out of the Old City. He drove slowly; his bike traced a wide arc and was apparently well under control. The arc widened and he drove up onto the sidewalk—to park, I assumed.

Did he have to park so close?

The motorbike fouled the air. The buzzing grew to a roar, burning my ears. I turned to face the man and his machine. Dark glasses hid his eyes. He was heading straight for me. I stepped out of his way, pressing my ribs into the fence by the river. He turned some more—deliberately, I think. The front tire spun off my ankle. The machine ploughed into my thigh. I screamed. My leg felt as if it had been slugged hard above the knee and branded above my sandal-clad foot. The police officer brought his motorcycle to a neat halt beside me. He got off and began fiddling with his blasted machine. I stood on one leg, against the fence by the river, with my left limb quivering in mid-air. For a moment, only the Barada wrinkled the silence.

Then passersby, all male, gathered round me. A dozen men clucked over my ankle. I was afraid to look. The men spoke of a hospital. I whimpered "no" and started to cry.

"Yes, yes. A hospital. He will take you," they said, pointing at the police officer who was fussing over his motorcycle.

The tears were still coming, but my "no" became stronger.

"In a car, in a car. He will take you in a car."

There was more buzzing. Two police officers showed up, following the path of their colleague—without hitting any pedestrians. There was talk I couldn't understand. Licking a tear into my mouth and letting their words blur around me, I looked down at my ankle, still hovering in mid-air below the hem of my skirt. There was some blood, but not much, and no bones poking out. The tire had spun off my leg, taking hair and flesh with it, leaving an angry raw burn across the front of my ankle. There were too many men around for me to pull up my skirt for a visual inspection of my leg above the knee. I ran my fingers over the cloth, cupping my palm over what felt like the beginnings of a camel hump swelling my thigh. The khaki cloth of my skirt wasn't stained with blood; the fabric hadn't snagged on any bone splinters. There was hope. The tears dried on my cheeks.

Meanwhile, public pressure, or more likely that of his peers, had convinced the police officer to acknowledge his victim, ending his fascination with his motorcycle. He didn't apologize or express any concern for my well-being, yet he was willing to hire a car to take me to a hospital. I refused.

The passersby were dismayed. "It's okay. He is police!"

I jerked my head back, adamantly. I couldn't bring myself to look at the man, much less go anywhere with him.

"Where will you go? Can you walk? You must stand on your foot," they said.

That was true. I could hardly walk away without lowering my foot to the sidewalk. Steeling my face, I straightened my left leg and touched my foot to the ground. Gradually I put more weight on it, easing away from the fence.

"*Malesh*," I said. Never mind. Ignoring the police officers, I thanked everyone else. Then, turning my back on the Barada, I walked slowly out of the sun and into the shade—doing my damnedest not to limp.

With every step, pain bit into my ankle and thigh. The rancid taste of stale fear coated my mouth. I felt tired and

149

vulnerable, and needed a place to rest. A mosque, propping up the heavens with a minaret patterned in peacock blues and greens, was a refuge. Sunlight shot the floor of its courtyard to a brilliant white. The square was so bright it seemed to slap at my eyes.

In exchange for a few lire, a grizzled caretaker gave me a black polyester cloak. After shrugging it over my clothes and hiding my hair under its hood, I was clothed as modestly as Islam required. A covered walkway skirting the courtyard offered a banner of shade which picnickers had claimed. I removed my sandals and took the shortest route to the entrance of the mosque: with a burning leg, I scuttled across the white-hot square.

A man at a table by the door sold five-inch cotton streamers in green, the colour of paradise for Muslims. In the centre of the mosque, under vaulted arches covered in stalactites of silver foil bent to shine like the sun, was a mausoleum enclosed in a golden grate. The grate was shaggy with strips of green. The cloth seller told me it was the tomb of Sayyida Ruqayya.

"Who is she?" I asked, betraying my ignorance.

"She is the daughter of Ali."

I nodded. The daughter of Ali, son-in-law of the Prophet Mohammed and the divinely inspired leader, the first *Imam*, of Shiite Muslims. I had inadvertently stumbled into a shrine for the Shiite sect—the official religion of Iran.

On one side of the holy tomb swarthy men in dark pants and long-sleeved shirts chanted, slapping their chests rhythmically. A man with a bushy black moustache led the chant with his face and arms raised up to the glittery heavens. On the other side of the tomb, voluntarily segregated, a throng of black and paisley sheets pitched and swayed as women shaped like parabolas tied green streamers to the grate.

No one took much notice of me. Sitting down on the carpet behind a group of women who had finished praying, I surreptitiously examined the florid camel hump on my thigh.

The bruise felt hot and spongy. I found a bandage in my day pack and plastered it over a bubble of blood below my ankle, leaving the tire burn untouched. Tucking my arms behind me, I pressed my wrists against the marble wall. Ice trickled into my veins. I closed my eyes, shutting out the glitter of the mosque. In the self-imposed darkness, voices in prayer funnelled into a howl like a winter storm on the Prairies. My thoughts were fractured. Sentences unravelled. *A police officer. In uniform. Motorcycle. Deliberate. On the sidewalk. Hit me. Why?* Why did I cross the street just then, just there? Why would a police officer run into me? Deliberately! I didn't understand it, couldn't understand it. Yet, sitting on the carpeted floor of a mosque, caught in a blizzard of devotion, I understood that in a Shiite shrine in Damascus—in a nest of believers—there could only be one explanation: God willed it.

At one corner of the tomb, a cross-eyed, toothless old woman rocked back and forth. Her knobby fingers tugged at her little piece of paradise. Her lips moved as she chanted prayers, and tears ran into the creases of her wrinkled face as she kissed and fondled the tomb of a woman who had been dead for more than a thousand years.

Later, outside the walls of the mosque, I wondered about Srouran (I never saw him again) and I wondered about the *mukhabarat*. Had I overestimated the power of a Canadian pass-port and the decency of the *mukhabarat*? Or was I simply in the wrong place at the wrong time? Travellers depend on guardian angels. In the week since my lover's departure, I had inadver-tently bullied a *mukhabarat* agent into showing me his ID in a deserted traffic circle in Quneitra; the felafel from the food stand in Khan Arnabah had emptied my stomach and bowels; I had spent a virtually sleepless night in an unlocked room in a scuzzy hotel in Dara'a; the car ride with Srouran, a creep who thought handcuffs and a club were nothing, had scared the heck out of me; and then, within half an hour of saying good-bye to Srouran outside the *Souq Saruja*, I was the victim of an "accident" orchestrated by a police officer. My confidence was shaken.

But I couldn't let that put me off travelling. I bandaged my ankle and made a day trip to Bosra to see the black basalt Roman theatre (the reason I had gone to Dara'a) which holds fifteen thousand spectators. Then I went north to Hama.

As for my leg, now, more than a year later, there is a scar on my ankle and an indentation in my thigh. A trough. A sinkhole. My fingers dip into a hollow where the camel hump bruise used to be. Courtesy of the police department in Damascus, I have a souvenir of Syrian authority built into my leg.

◈ travellers

Transient pods holed up in hotels, speaking of elsewhere, not home, not here. Flashing their medals, a traveller's trophy, passports blotted, stamps of ink. Speak of where others have not been.

Hama, a religiously conservative city, is infamous for a brutal crackdown in February 1982 after members of the outlawed Muslim Brotherhood ambushed government troops performing a raid in the ancient quarter and "liberated" the city. President Assad's troops moved in and flattened parts of Hama. House-to-house searches followed and there were reports of mass executions. According to Amnesty International, the uprising and the crackdown that followed killed an estimated 10,000 to 25,000 people. Hama, situated on the Orontes River, *Nahr al-Assi*—the rebel river, is also famous for its norias, giant wooden water wheels used for irrigation for centuries. Now boys use them as ferris wheel diving platforms. The water wheels moan like doors in a haunted house.

My guidebook said the Cairo Hotel in Hama was "spot-lessly clean" and when I arrived, a barefoot man was actually washing the floor. The Cairo Hotel was popular with independent travellers and the friendly proprietor put me in a room with two Dutch women on a three-week holiday. One of the women was a nurse, and she cleaned the tire burn on my leg and bandaged it up properly. The Dutch women and a Belgian man they had befriended were quiet, curious travellers—unlike some of the other guests, who casually plunked the names of faraway places into every conversation as if to say geographic credentials are the only ones that matter on the road.

At breakfast one morning I struggled with a slab of feta cheese, trying to cut it lengthwise to make thinner slices. An Englishman sat down beside me. From the other side of the breakfast room, a crisp Australian accent called out, "You wouldn't do that in Iran."

The speaker, a tall, loose-knit fellow, popped a black olive into his mouth. The Englishman raised his eyebrows slightly and helped himself to pita bread, butter, and apricot jam. I wondered if there were laws about cutting feta cheese.

Pfft. The Australian spat the stone into his hand and flicked it onto a saucer before continuing. "Sit down beside a woman. You wouldn't just sit down by a woman like that in Iran."

"Then thank goodness we're in Syria," said the Englishman.

An American woman—a big-eyed, braless blonde who, with bare arms and legs had more flesh exposed than street-walkers I had seen in Damascus—asked the Australian about Iran. After travelling there for a month, he had many interesting stories. He stayed at the Cairo Hotel for two days and talked of nothing but Iran. I wondered if he had any room left for Syria.

One evening a young New Zealand man named James came into the sitting room. He had visited a number of places in the southern part of the country and he listed the names as if reading an awards list. I was tired of galloping travellers who zing from place to place, collecting geographic names like trophies, as if a long list of names will confirm that one has really seen a country. James didn't mention Quneitra, and in a moment of childish obnoxiousness, I seized on it. His response was, "Quneitra?"

"The Golan Heights."

He hadn't gone to Quneitra. With an air of authority, he informed me that one needed a special permit which was impossible to get in under a week. It really was not feasible.

"Are you kidding? It takes five minutes! It took me longer to find the office than it did to get the permit."

"Really." His voice was flat. He wanted to change the subject, I could see that, but I wasn't in a generous mood so I rattled on about Quneitra and the Golan Heights for a while. By the time I shut up, I felt hollow and ridiculous, annoyed with myself for getting caught up in the hierarchical games that travellers play.

James was staring at the map of Syria in his guidebook. The Golan Heights, which were marked as being under Israeli or U.N. control, were at the bottom of the page, in the southwest corner of the country. We were in Hama, closer to the northern frontier at the top of the page. The Golan Heights looked far away.

Under his breath, more to himself than to me, James muttered, "Damn. I'd like to have gone there. Just to say I was there."

I silently condemned him for being so shallow. But the towering walls of superiority crumbled all too soon. What were my motives? I asked myself. Why did I bring up Quneitra? Black waters swirl beneath the ice of brittle conversations.

That day I had hired a driver to take me to a first-century castle that wasn't in the guidebook. Leaving the driver in the van at the foot of the hill, I hiked up to the castle—a basalt victory soars out of a limestone moat on a barren conical hill— and stormed the fortress. In the circle of broken walls, the wind moaned. A falcon disappeared into the belly of a bottomless cistern and I went down on my knees to gingerly peer into darkness. I love having ruins to myself. I thought I could feel the spirits—the falcon coming home.

After a while the driver came up, as I expected he might, and I met him on the rim of the moat in a spot where we could be seen from the Bedouin tents on the plain below.

"Why do you want to visit this?" He sneered at the stones. "There is nothing."

"It's old and interesting." The wind flapped at my skirt.

"There is nothing." With downturned lips and a wave of his arm, he brushed off the castle.

On the way back to the van he claimed the fee we had agreed on didn't cover the return trip. We weren't more than a mile off the main road and once I got that far, I figured I could easily flag down a *meecro*, but when he saw that I was prepared to walk, he drove me back to town at no extra charge.

I told other travellers about Qalaat ash-Shamamis, yet I didn't mention it to James. He could have Quneitra if he were willing to backtrack, but Qalaat ash-Shamamis was too close. I didn't want the Fortress of the Sun to be just another castle on his I-was-there list. Perhaps I wanted to protect the spirits. I didn't think a man like James would understand them. The falcon didn't belong on anybody's mantle.

◈ *sightseeing*

I left Hama early. It was supposed to be a two-castle day trip. A *meecro* van let me out at a side road that led up the hill to the first castle. I started walking up the hill, but had to stop four times to decline ride offers from men on motor scooters. My ankle hadn't finished healing yet and a motor scooter veering towards me seemed like a menace. Finally I accepted an offer from a family in a truck. I hopped into the back with the children and gave them all pens. The truck dropped me off at the entrance to Qalaat al-Mudiq. The castle took over the site of an acropolis; a village took over the castle. Thirteenth-century fortress walls have modern windows and balconies.

I drank tea with three Muslim women in a stone house with a turquoise door. The belly-dancing antics of Sana, their eight-year-old sister, had us laughing hysterically. A teenage brother was trying to sleep on a foam pad on the floor.

Al-Mudiq (the former acropolis) and the ruins of Aphamea are separated by fields of sunflowers with heart-shaped leaves and Fibonacci faces. Cleopatra and Mark Anthony visited Aphamea when peacock and hunting scene mosaics were shiny and new. Lion tearing at cow, gazelle, goat, donkey; blood pouring from the victim's neck. Now the mosaics are stacked in a museum. Faded puzzles missing pieces.

There were no other tourists at Aphamea that morning. The ruins were mine, all mine. Alone on the Great Colonnade! The columns lining the ancient street were a slalom course for swallows. I was alone with my thoughts and the birds.

Put-put-put.

Once there were chariots; now a motor scooter was on the Great Colonnade. A well-built Arab man ruined my solitude. For what? The usual questions about marriage and babies and whether I had a problem. Why was it always the woman? "My *husband* has a problem," I lied. "He can't have children."

The man flinched and looked away. I watched him squirm.

"Where is he, your husband?"

Canada was too far away. "He's in Hama."

"Why not here?"

"He's sick."

"Why you not with him?"

"I'm not sick." It was a stupid thing to say, especially after casting doubt on a man's virility. I might just as well have said I eat pickled babies. His eyes flared and outrage scuttled across his face. Yet the storm passed quickly.

"My wife never goes out alone," he said quietly before getting down to business.

The man, who was about thirty, had Roman coins for sale. I didn't want any. He offered to show me the tombs of Roman soldiers. It was too far to walk, I could ride on the back of his motor scooter, he said. First the tombs, then we could make love.

I rebuked him with an indignant "I am married!"

His response: "Me too!"

I stomped off into a patch of thistles because I figured an

insult to my honour demanded a bit of high drama. The *put-put-put* faded as the man disappeared. Bumblebees filled the void. A handsome man, I thought. Had he been a little more likable, in my wild years, I might have accepted everything he had offered. As it was, I never found the tombs.

Qalaat Sheizar was on my agenda for the afternoon. After a picnic lunch of cucumbers and tomatoes on flat round bread, I caught a *meecro* from al-Mudiq to Sheizar.

Qalaat Sheizar is a ragged mediaeval fortress crouched on the brow of a hill. A band of scruffy children met me in the village below the castle. Six snot-faced little children with BIG JABBERING voices. *Ben, ben, stilo, stilo.* What did they want pens for? Were they all writing novels? Grubby hands plucked at my clothes. A boy tugged at the zipper on my day pack. I roared. They backed off. A bit. Crossing the Orontes River, a girl took a run at me and tried to push me off the bridge. There were no guard rails.

A potato-faced man with a patchy moustache came and shooed the horrid children away. I told him my husband was in Hama and he nodded respectfully, and then took me to the river and sat me down in the water beside his mother, who had a hieroglyphic tattoo on her chin. The man had never crossed paths with tourists before, so he treated me like a Syrian woman: my honour was worth protecting.

I dubbed my rescuer and his extended family the Woolwashers because the women—his mother, sister, sister-in-laws, and his two wives—sat in the river, soaping, kneading, paddling, and rinsing wool. An empty water jug was a drum and they sang while they worked. Thirty or more children—angelic children—darted about, playing. The men stood on the grassy shore. The air was filled with the sounds of a drum beat, singing, and laughter, and the smell of the river, soap, and wet wool.

When the women finished washing the wool, they waded into the middle of the river where the water was waist-deep and splashed around a bit. A young man, the husband of one of the women, swam in his pants and undershirt but the women just played. They probably didn't know how to swim. How would they learn? They wore baggy pants under two layers of long-sleeved dresses that reached to their toes. On a hot day, with all those clothes, no one deserved a refreshing dip more than they did. I watched the women from a rectangular rock, part of Qalaat Sheizar, in the shallow part of the river. Water swirled around my hips and gently tugged at my skirt. The women shrieked and laughed as they floated past me. They were having fun and I laughed with them, but at the same time I thought about how far apart our lives were. They would never know what it feels like to leave your clothes in a heap on the shore, to wade into delicious water, to feel it caress your thighs, to slip into a river the way a man slips into a woman, I imagine, then to float on your back, creating islands in the stream.

Of course, I didn't do any of that in the Orontes, either. I didn't even shed my money belt to swim fully dressed. Playing the prude, I stayed in shallow water, keeping my money belt just above the water line.

We ate *loonch* (the only English word I heard that afternoon) under a eucalyptus tree, tossing chicken bones, onion jackets, and green pepper innards over our shoulders. Floppy-eared goats picked up the scraps. The food was good and there was plenty of it. I had already eaten, yet I ate again—knowing full well that what's safe for the locals could destroy the health of a foreigner—because it would have been rude to refuse their food. I tried not to eat very much.

Then the women loaded the wool into three-wheeled, psychedelic, mosquito-like trucks, and we all piled in and the men drove—the only "work" I saw them do—to a village where the family lived in concrete houses. The women unloaded the wet wool and hung it on racks on the roof of one of the houses.

"*Wen khuroof?*" I asked. I didn't see any sheep.

Because they didn't have any. The men had bought the

160

wool at a market in Hama, they told me. Along with driving and protecting female honour just by being there, buying wool was men's work.

Inside the house, there were foam pads on the concrete floor, and a cabinet on one wall held colouring books. The room was childproof, which was a good thing because I counted sixteen children. All sat quietly, staring at me while the women served lime drinks on a tray. It was hot (damn hot) and I knew I was being foolhardy but I even sucked on the ice cubes.

A horse-faced woman, one of my rescuer's two wives, pulled back a paisley red scarf to show me gold earrings and a semicircle of gold coins on her forehead.

"Beautiful! Very beautiful."

"Where is your gold?" she asked. The woman's rough plough-like hands held a toddler with gold hearts in her earlobes, bangles on her wrist, and a string of blue beads looped around her neck. The child's white hands ran over a panel of red embroidery on her mother's heavy black robe, which was still wet from her work in the river.

I just shrugged and smiled. I wasn't wearing any jewellery.

The woman leaned forward and there was concern in her face. "No money?"

I was embarrassed. There was more money strapped around my waist than she might see in an entire year. I told her my gold was at home and hoped she wouldn't misinterpret the sudden colour in my face as shame.

She wanted me to stay the night but her husband told her my partner was in a hotel in Hama and I regretted the lie. Later he drove me to the main road to catch a *meecro* and insisted on paying my fare. Then he stood at the edge of the road and waved goodbye. The sun was low and he cast a long shadow in the strawberry light.

It wasn't a two-castle day because I never made it to the second castle, Qalaat Sheizar. Nothing happens as planned: that's what I love about independent travel. There's no tour bus, you're on your own, anything can happen. And I have to admit I always hope that something unplanned will.

Guidebooks are full of monuments and ruins because they stay put. I seek out stones—I have pictures of castles I can no longer identify—to connect with people. The people who quarried the stones, built the walls, carved inscriptions, walked under the archways, drew water from the cisterns. The people who dismantled the walls, the people who live in the shadow of the past, making it part of the present. It's people I remember. Random encounters. Paths crossing. Tangents. I'm intrigued by fragments of lives. Mosaics. Splinters of myself, and splinters of others caught in the snare of my memory. I sent the Woolwashers and the women in al-Mudiq copies of photographs I took that day.

◉ *a damn good place*

You could sleep on the roof of the Cairo Hotel in Hama for the equivalent of a couple of bucks or you could take a bed in a shared room for not much more, and it was clean compared to other "bottom end" hotels. There were two pit toilets and one throne toilet and they all worked. The Cairo Hotel was a damn good place to be sick. I should have stayed there longer.

After three days of being tethered to the toilets, I was tired of waiting for an illness (almost certainly triggered by the generosity of the Woolwashers and my willingness to accept it) to run its course. Three days of drinking watered-down ginger ale and munching on soft biscuits while rationing the Naguib Mahfouz novel I was reading. In the evenings I made a carefully timed dash to the restaurant in a five-star hotel where I paid top dollar for European food, though I wasn't hungry. When a Belgian traveller commented that he had known me for three days and that I had lost weight since he'd known me, I decided to give up on letting my bowels sort themselves out and took several of the chalky red tablets in my medical kit.

The following day, I declared myself well enough to travel, in spite of the fact that I had no appetite and Syrian food scared me. Two days later, after I had visited the fifth-century ruins of Saint Simeon's Cathedral and then headed east into the desert, my health gave out. I had swallowed the last of the chalky red tablets and I was in the desert—sick in the desert in July.

At the ruins of the walled city of Rasafah, in the desert southwest of Raqqa, the sun took on van Gogh proportions. It swallowed the sky and half the earth, which held the heat like a cast-iron pan on fire. Outside the walls of the ruined city were Bedouin tents and children with machine-gun voices. *Ben, ben, ben, ben, ben, ben, ben. P* is a stranger to Arabic.

Imshi. Go away. I have no pens. I am sick. Leave me alone. Go away.

The girls disappeared into the shadows of black tents spread like bat wings over the desert. The boys remained. *Madame! Madame!* Off to my left, twenty feet away. A laughing boy with his *galabiyya* crunched up under his chin. A naked body. Micturition. Golden arch, spattered dirt. The smell. The smell of dust and urine. I squawked, I charged; a crazy foreigner flapping chicken-bone arms. The boys scattered, zigzagged like soldiers; banshees running for cover.

The ancient city of Rasafah: gypsum walls in a flat, featureless land; fifth-century Byzantine corral for a jumbled basilica and underground banquet hall cisterns; the enclosed desert a war zone of pockmarks left by treasure-hunting vultures. The ruins, the ruins. I remember the smell of excrement—old and new. Latrines in the corners of dark rooms with low ceilings. The sound of flies fussing over the spread. The comfort of stone walls—my body searching for balance. Sun; heat; dust; cramps; flies . . . defecation. My heart slushing blood and tar through translucent arteries, rhubarb veins. The sun, the sun, that van Gogh sun swallowed a cloudless sky. Shade had a magnetic pull. No white peonies of hope bunched on the horizon. I had to get out of the desert.

In the village of al-Mansura, I waited for a bus to Aleppo. Placing his right hand on the chest pocket of his *galabiyya*, the ticket seller swore I was like a sister to him. He brought me a chair. A few minutes later I followed him to the courtyard of a private home. The pit toilet built into a corner of the courtyard didn't have a roof or a door; a floor, and mud walls on three-and-a-half sides were enough. On the way back to the main street, a shortcut took us through an alley strewn with hirsute legs and cloven hooves. Goat remnants. Decomposing. The stench made my stomach heave. I nearly threw up.

On the bus to Aleppo, I sat behind the driver, willing him to go faster and faster, to pass on blind corners and bang on the horn, to blast offending vehicles out of our way: I wanted him to do all the things I had cursed every other driver in Syria for. Aleppo was three hours away; the fuse on my bowels was half that length—if I was lucky! At one point I was ready to beg, bribe, or bludgeon the driver to stop the bus when, of his own accord, he pulled into a village for a break. A five minute rest stop. I have seldom been so grateful for anything in my life.

In Aleppo I spent three nights in a room just slightly bigger than a stack of coffins. I had no interest in food, but one must eat in order to stay alive. In the dining room of a fine hotel, I had corn flakes and orange juice for breakfast; in the evenings I pecked at spaghetti or chicken in upscale restaurants featuring European cuisine. The meals, which I could never finish, cost more than my hotel room.

As soon as I was well enough to appreciate my surroundings, I followed the footsteps of Lawrence of Arabia and Dames Agatha Christie and Freya Stark into the faded elegance of the Baron Hotel. Room 205 in the southeast corner of the hotel had a tall window with a rounded top like a tombstone. French doors opened onto a balcony in the south. The room had two armchairs with antique peonies blooming on russet cushions; a wardrobe with a full-length mirror lamenting light lost in a maze of shadows; a straight-backed chair; a writing desk with an embroidered runner; a modern electric fan; an antique desk phone right out of a movie set; and a coat rack which I decked in lemon-scented laundry. The bathtub was grand, the towels luxurious. I fell asleep at night in a soft double bed, listening to wind rustle eucalyptus leaves. In the morning I awoke to car horns and the clip-clop of hooves on pavement, and through the half-moon dome of the eastern window, the sun poured champagne crystals of light. The Baron Hotel in Aleppo was a damn good place to be on the mend.

◉ *sanity & saints*

Early in the fifth century, a thirteen-year-old shepherd named Simeon had a vision that prompted him to enter a Christian monastery in northwestern Syria. Life in the monastery was intended to be arduous, but Simeon pushed the limits: a spiked girdle, designed to draw blood; a summer in the garden, buried up to his neck. The monks found such zealous masochism disturbing, and they dismissed him from the monastery.

In 423 A.D. Simeon moved to the top of a ten-foot pole. Gradually increasing the height, he finally settled on top of a sixty-foot pillar, no more than six feet across, where he spent the last thirty years of his life. To ensure that he wouldn't fall, he wore an iron collar shackled to a metal railing. Twice a day he preached to pilgrims, though he refused to speak to women, even turning away his own mother. In July of 459, Simeon died at home, some sixty feet above the earth. A cathedral was built around his pillar, and it was, at the time, the largest church in the world.

Fifteen centuries later, I visited the ruins of Saint Simeon's

Cathedral. Wishbone arches frame stark images of boulder-clad hills and bend the sky. The pillar is gone. Centuries of souvenir-hunting pilgrims carried it away, chip by chip. Touching the base, the pedestal on which Simeon's pillar had stood, and looking up into a clear blue sky, I could imagine him far above me: shaggy silhouette against the sun; an unwashed man ranting and raving; around his neck, a collar and a chain like a string of besmirched bubbles.

I laughed out loud and shuddered, trying to push him out of my mind, out of the crumbling remains of a cathedral built in his honour. Poor Simeon, I thought. Yet, the little shepherd boy was lucky. He was born at the right time, for those were the good old days when a madman could become a saint. We wouldn't be so kind today.

◉ trees

Trees in the foothills of southwestern Alberta are windblown antlers that spike the buttes without blocking the view of the Rockies, which rise like ragged beaks of prehistoric bluebirds pecking holes in the sky. A few trees clutter river valleys and creek bottoms; every summer cottonwoods burst into fluffy tears. But for the most part, in Alberta the hills are bare, covered in bunch grass and rough fescue. I grew up on that land—not good soil for trees, but perfect grazing ground for cattle. The Rockies crumple into prairies and the sky goes on forever.

Later, as a young adult, I lived in eastern Ontario, steeped in the majesty of maples and oaks. It seems laughable now, but I spent at least two of the seven years I lived there resenting the leafy wooden blots on what others thought were beautiful landscapes. I couldn't appreciate the pulchritude of a tree-filled vista till one fall: the colours of autumn made the trees look like fireballs and pumpkins; I kept a scrapbook of leaves—ginkgo, catalpa, buckeye, horse chestnut—and fell in love with trees.

In Syria, I would wait beside an interesting tree—one with strange fruit, fragrant flowers, eccentric leaves, or spotted bark—until I could find someone, usually more than a little puzzled, to identify it and write its name on a piece of paper. *Zatoon, difly, keena, ruman, toota.* After a struggle with my Arabic-English dictionary, I discovered olive, oleander, eucalyptus, pomegranate, mulberry.

You never know when the words you learn may be useful. I was walking in the countryside near Kafroon when a Christian family, relaxing outside their house, waved for me to join them. We sat on wooden stools under a mulberry tree, drinking the darkened blood of its berries. Their milk cow grazed nearby. Orchards turned the valley below us into a basket of jewels.

We spoke of trees and they were curious about my homeland.

"Do you have mulberry trees in Canada?" they asked.

"No."

"Plum trees?"

"No." I forgot that there are.

"Pomegranate trees?"

"No."

"Olive trees?"

"No."

After a moment of silence, the mother—a woman as plump and full of life as any fruit tree—asked, "What kind of trees do you have in Canada?"

They looked at me expectantly and I wanted to tell them about saskatoons, to give them the aroma, the taste of my mother's pies fresh from the oven. Instead I sat there dumb, as if my mouth were full of chokecherries, tart and sour. I didn't know the words for saskatoon, chokecherry, maple, horse chestnut, or oak. I tried to draw the leaves; my fingers failed me.

When we had finished our drinks, I showed them some

photographs that I often carried with me. They looked with dismay at the coppery skin and peeling red bark of an arbutus tree on the rocky coast of British Columbia. Then I showed them pictures of my family's cattle ranch in Alberta. The foothills were yellow like the flanks of a cougar. "No trees!" the mother said softly, and I could see from the look on her face that she thought Canada must be a barren land.

▨ *Kafroon*

When Syrians speak of Kafroon, it is as if they are speaking of the sweetest, most succulent fruit on this planet.

Kafroon is a quiet village in the lush mountains that run along the Syrian coast of the Mediterranean. Its roads are lined with pomegranates and plums. There is no traffic to speak of and there are no calls to the mosque. It is a Christian enclave where women have hair and waists and cleavage.

I went there in July to recover from the illness brought on by the kindness of the Woolwashers and to hide from the summer heat that pressed so hard on the rest of Syria. There is nothing listed on the tourist agenda for Kafroon: no castles, no citadel, no ruins. That was a relief.

Instead of sightseeing, I sat at a table under willow trees beside a clear stream where fish jumped, leaving orbital rings in the water. A young boy in a crisp white shirt, a navy blue vest and shorts, stood in the stream, water puckering at his ankles.

His sister sat on a chair, almost drowned in lace ruffles. Trolling with a cut-off water bottle on a wire, the boy scooped up six little fish and placed them at my feet. His father threw the fish back into the stream.

In an outdoor cafe, I smeared *baba ghanouj* (mashed egg-plant and sesame seeds) on pita bread, and after a week with no interest in food, savoured every bite as if it were caviar.

The sun set behind hills of olive trees. In the shadows of dusk, trees dotted the ground like puffs of smoke. When the sun disappeared, it was chilly, like summer nights in Alberta. I put on the sweater I had thought I would never need. A donkey brayed and I listened to frogs debate their destiny.

I slept more hours than I could believe.

When I returned to Damascus, the woman at the Poste Restante wicket in the main post office asked me where I had been, and I spoke of Kafroon as if I had eaten a succulent fruit—the sweetest, most succulent fruit on this planet.

✣ books

Before leaving Canada, I read Freya Stark's *Letters from Syria*, a delightful account of studying Arabic in what's now Lebanon, being sick in Damascus, and a donkey trek in the Hauran area of southern Syria in the 1920s. Friends loaned me *Among the Believers: an Islamic Journey* by V.S. Naipaul, and gave me *Nine Parts of Desire: the Hidden World of Islamic Women* by Geraldine Brooks, and *Indiscreet Journeys*, an anthology of travel writing edited by Lisa St. Aubin de Terán.

When I arrived in Damascus I was deep inside *The Republic of Love* by Carol Shields. A grubby hotel room near the Takieh as-Sulaymanieh Mosque became Winnipeg as Fay McLeod and Tom Avery fell in love. In the lobby, under the brown-eyed plastic gaze of President Assad, I turned the final pages with tears in my eyes as I waited for my landlord to take me to the little house.

My landlady, Offa, loaned me *Politically Correct Bedtime Stories: Modern Tales for our Life and Times* by James Finn Garner, which belonged to her "adopted son" Dave. The rest of his books were religious and I had no interest in them. Huda loaned me the only English book she had, *Men in the Sun*, powerful short stories of desperation and displacement, and my introduction to the Palestinian author Ghassan Kanafani.

Then I had a problem. Travellers barter books, but I wasn't meeting any travellers because I lived in a house, not a hotel. A few shops, mostly in the big hotels, sold English books, but the prices were beyond my budget. I used birthday money from my sister to splurge on *Guide to SYRIA* by Afif Bahnassi.

Huda suggested I join the Assad Library, an air-conditioned oasis of sparkling chandeliers and shiny mosaics. A set of Canadian encyclopaedias gave me a flush of patriotic pride. In another set of encyclopaedias, under the entry for Alberta I found a picture of a two-grain-elevator village. My hometown, Cowley. The same photograph was once featured on a postage stamp.

I read Freya Stark's *Baghdad Sketches* for the second time in the reading room of the Assad Library, because even with a photo ID library card, which you had to show to get past the machine gun at the gate, you weren't allowed to take books home.

The German books at the Goethe Institute weren't guarded by a machine gun, but I wasn't allowed to borrow them, either, because I only had a tourist visa. I browsed through books about *Damaskus* and then chastised myself for reading about it in a sterile German library rather than living the real thing outside the door. The only reminders that I was in Syria, not Hessen, were young Arab men poring over the pictures in *Stern*, muffled calls to the mosque, and a world map with a hole in the Mediterranean where the word Israel had been.

Finally Offa showed me the American Library Club, a small room redolent of books, books, books. Books I could borrow—I felt as if I'd struck gold. *A Passage to India* by E.M. Forster; *The Prime of Miss Jean Brodie* by Muriel Spark; and *An*

Episode of Sparrows by Rumer Godden. I recommended *How to Live with Another Person* by David Viscott, M.D., to my lover.

Colin Thubron's *Mirror to Damascus* made me wonder whether there was any place in the Old City where someone hadn't been murdered or raped. In 1860 a Muslim mob had massacred Christian men and there were reports of women being driven through the streets naked before being sold to Bedouin. How awful, I thought, until I met the handsome Bedouin who tossed mutton onto my plate at the Desert Festival.

Then Margaret Atwood's *Wilderness Tips* (too much infidelity—not a good book to read when your lover is far away); and *The Woman Warrior: Memoirs of a girlhood among ghosts* by Maxine Hong Kingston. I passed over a biography of Sylvia Plath (because I had a gas stove) in favour of Maya Angelou's *Wouldn't Take Nothing for My Journey Now*.

In Africa, Isak Dinesen, the Baroness Karen Blixen, read a book worth reading the way the author would have liked his book read. She likened a good read to being transported. Sitting on a wooden chair in the kitchen of a little house in Damascus, with my right arm resting on the stove and my feet up on the windowsill, *Out of Africa* and *Shadows on the Grass* by Isak Dinesen took me to the dark continent. And *The Shipping News* by E. Annie Proulx took me to Newfoundland. I read slowly, wanting fresh salty air to mask the smell of the gas stove and the drain.

The American Library Club was open two mornings a week. One Thursday, I went to return *Syria: a tourist's guide* by Fuad Shaban and to take out another book, only to discover that because of the Muslim *Eid al-Adha*, Festival of the Sacrifice, which begins on the last day of the *Hajj*, the Pilgrimage to Mecca, the library was closed. Not only were sheep being slaughtered in the streets, the post office was closed, there were no pastries in the pastry shops, and the library wouldn't open again until Tuesday. I could have cried. I reread *Syria: a tourist's guide* and called Offa who found me *An Ideal Husband* by Oscar Wilde.

When the library reopened, I borrowed *Anatomy of Eve* by Leopold Stein, M.D., with Martha Alexander; and *A Damsel in Distress* by P.G. Wodehouse.

One morning I waited for a nearly empty bus to fill. The driver, a man with a nose like a bronc, stood in the shade, shouting: *"Suweida, Suweida."* Within a few minutes the bus was half full. It was hot, damn hot. My legs felt sticky; sweat ran down the backs of knees. The forecast high was for forty-some degrees. Ruins, I thought, mosaics and ruins on a brutally hot day. Was I crazy? When the bus was two passengers short of a full load, I bolted. I got to the library ten minutes before closing and booked *A Passage to Egypt: the Life of Lucie Duff Gordon* by Katherine Frank. A cool shower. Then, with the fan on high, the Nile flowed through my living room.

My lover supplied me with *The Thief and the Dogs* and *Miramar* by Naguib Mahfouz; and I bartered for *Summer's Lease* by John Mortimer and *Sleeping Murder: Miss Marple's Last Case* by Agatha Christie.

Page by page, I rationed and savoured the words of every precious book.

I left Syria in the company of *Murther and Walking Spirits* by Robertson Davies.

✸ *farewell*

Time the conveyor belt moves us forward whether we like it or not.

How do you leave a country? To fly is to flee—it happens too fast. I studied the map. I could stay on the ground, cut across a green border, drive into another land with my face up against a pane of glass—to roll into the arms of another lover, wooed by another foreign tongue. That, too, would be a form of flight. I want to leave slowly, I thought. I want to float away.

Offa presented me with an olive-wood box inlaid with mother-of-pearl triangles, stars, diamonds, and hexagons. An arabesque puzzle, a riddle, a maze—a tissue box lined with red velvet. "When you cry or …" she held one hand to her bulbous nose and snorted, "think of me. Think of Damascus." A tissue box full of memories.

My camera became my eyes. I wanted to record everything, to capture life in Damascus on multicoloured rectangular scraps. A tall order. Life isn't captured so easily. The woman at the Poste Restante wicket and a man selling cactus treats didn't want their pictures taken. Neither did my neighbour, a fat man, who sat on a stool outside his carpentry shop while his son did all the work. But President Assad banners didn't mind. I took street shots, freezing bodies in the summer heat and flattening curves and angles into two-dimensional submission, leaving out traffic noise and the smell of exhaust fumes overpowered by jasmine. I snapped my way through downtown. *Click click click* . . . Damascus was a string of red beads trickling through my fingers.

I took my camera to the market, *Souq al-Hamidiyyah,* where a young man named Ibrahim fell into step beside me. I knew him a bit because he had tried to lure me into his shop on other occasions. He had a cloudy left eye. I showed him my camera and told him I had only come to take pictures.

"You can take pictures from my shop," he said, pointing at a second-floor balcony draped in Bedouin dresses. I couldn't resist. Into a side alley, up a flight of stairs, through his tiny shop, and we were on the balcony, looking down at the *souq. Click click click.* I finished a film, though I doubted my flash could illuminate the shadows. A boy delivered glasses of sugary tea and we drank it in Ibrahim's shop. Actually, his father's shop. Ibrahim was only twenty-two. He suggested we meet to go swimming.

"I'm leaving tomorrow," I said.

He suggested we meet that evening.

I trotted out my invisible 'husband'.

Ibrahim lamented that all the foreign women said they had boyfriends or husbands. "They only want to be friends with me, but after some time they sleep with somebody else." He wasn't being pushy or fresh. He was just lamenting.

Then the sales pitch began: silver earrings, malachite necklaces, mother-of-pearl inlaid backgammon boards and pencil cases, kaftans, silk vests, embroidered tablecloths, dama-scene brocades, Bedouin dresses. I had seen it all before in other shops, and although I agreed that everything Ibrahim showed me was very beautiful, I didn't want to buy anything. But what Ibrahim didn't seem to know about dealing with women, he did know about sales pitches: persistence might pay off. After turning down nearly everything in the store, gold leaf waves riding a smouldering green glitter twist seduced me. I bought a dress that captured the spirit of Damascus better than my camera lens could.

I packed notebooks of Arabic squiggles; maps; brochures; scribblers; journals; linen tablecloths matted with swirls of embroidered flowers; cassettes of Fayrouz from Lebanon and Um Kulthoum from Egypt (the Syrians I asked were unable to recommend a local singer); a Ministry of Tourism calendar featuring a glossy year of musical instruments; and the Syrian dress of gold leaf waves riding a smouldering green glitter twist. I packed up fragments of life in a city of jasmine, fountains, and gardens, and sent them to my lover in Canada.

The last morning, any morning in the wee house in Damascus. Chocolate croissants and peppermint tea for break-fast. I ate in the kitchen, with my feet up on the windowsill. Doves with delicate vase-like features whirred on the balcony. The sun was behind the mosque. *Allah akbar!* Surreal echoes came from every corner of the city. I could smell the gas stove and the drain. A feather duster in a woman's hand, shaking, shaking from a fifth-floor window of an apartment building across the street. Particles of dust rained on the courtyard below. *Haleeb, haleeb*—the hoarse shouts of a boy selling bottled milk I didn't dare drink. The gas man's *clang, clang*—a wrench banged on a metal canister.

Everything was magnified.

Clarified.

We seldom live in the present. Routines are ignored until they're about to be broken, violated, abandoned.

The wall clock tapped out time like a snare drum.

At eight o'clock on the evening of the day my final tourist visa expired, a ship sailed out of the harbour at Lattakia on the Mediterranean coast of Syria. Waves rippled the shoreline. On the far side of a widening sheet of inky blue water, beyond a curtain of mountains, under a billion stars masquerading as diamonds, after four months in Syria, I was leaving behind a home.

I stood on the deck, gazing at mountains unspooled on the eastern horizon. The mainland receded until gradually distance swallowed what darkness wouldn't.

At the foot of a mountain, Jebel Qassioun, the al-Ghutah oasis ripples the desert for the city of jasmine, *Dimashq*, to endure. I had settled a while in Damascus.